The Black Holocaust

50 million died on slave ships
Millions die in captivity
Identities stolen

The Freedom to Murder African Americans

Timothy White, Sr.

Dedication

I dedicate this book to the memories of those families who suffered at the hands of the slave masters and survived. It was because of their efforts, blood, sweat and tears that African Americans today can overcome adversity, anger, resentment, and threats of death.

Their history, resolve, strength, and faith are what drives and motivates me to stop and examine what I was told as truths. I stepped out to go in search of the truth. It is in their honor and their memory that I wrote this book.

I extend a special dedication to those who helped to support this effort.

Timothy White, Sr.

Edited by: Patricia A. Perry

Introduction

There have been many books written about black people and their fight for equality, and justice. Over the centuries, it was believed that things would change for them, but looking back the struggle continues.

This is not a book about black history, but includes history that has often been overlooked by blacks and whites alike. I have not set out in this book to do an in depth account of the events that have become a part of American history.

It is your responsibility to do your part in this process of learning your own history. Schools do not teach or give the whole story. We now live in the age of information where the availability of research via the World Wide Web is at our fingertips. Things that have been hidden in the past have come to the light.

For those who seek the truth, the truth is out there. The danger is once you know the truth you cannot go back and undue or erase it. Some have tried and will continue to do so.

Information reduces ignorance, and it can also give or restore power to all who sincerely seek it. It is our past that guides our present day actions. What occurred yesterday impacts today. We have been told that if we do not remember the things done in our past, then we are doomed to repeat them.

This book is about what was done to a race of people who did nothing more than to be born of another race; how they suffered because of their color; how they were imported to a strange land and brutalized. Was the purpose to help them fit into a culture, or to become civilized?

This book takes an unsettling look at the ways of white America and the deeds done to its African American people for the sake of progress and economical development. A look at what it cost people of color for the advancement of this nation. Even as I write this book and talk about the dark past of American slavery, there are still those oppressed, who continue to be held captive to spiritual slavery and a Jim Crow mentality.

There are those who refuse to believe slavery ever happened. At the very least, it was not what black people want the rest of the world to believe it was. There are still organizations fighting against the rights of blacks to exist. The fight for freedom continues.

Of course there are some who will say that this is an old matter and why bring it up at all. Then there are those who play the blame game finger pointing, and still others who say do not hold them accountable for what happened in the past. The point of this book is not about blame, but shame. America should be ashamed of itself for what it did to other human beings just because of their color.

Chapters

Dedication

Presidents and Slavery

Introduction

1	America the Brutal
16	Black Owned
23	Born Disadvantaged
33	Genesis
42	Black Holocaust
53	The Bible and Slavery
62	Tolerance is not Acceptance
72	Blacks and White Movies
85	Only the Strong Survived
91	They're Only children
101	Black Codes
109	Blacks History
120	Enemy at Home
134	Kings and Queens
148	See No Evil
170	Till Death
161	They Can't Handle the Truth
I-II	Read Me
i-vi	Emancipation Proclamation
vii-xix	Declaration of Independence
xx-xxix	The Fugitive Slave Act
	Illustrations/Photos
	Conclusion

Presidents and Slavery

Bill Clinton said, "Going back to the time before we were a nation, European Americans received the fruits of the slave trade and we were wrong in that."

John Adams said, "Negro slavery is an evil of colossal magnitude."

President Bush called slavery "one of the greatest crimes of history."

The slave owner **James Monroe** called the international slave trade "abominable."

John Quincy Adams in 1820 called slavery "the great and foul stain upon the North American union."

Even though he was a slave-owning president, **James Madison** called slavery an "evil' and a dreadful calamity." "God knows that I detest slavery, but it is an existing evil, for which we are not responsible, and we must endure it."

Andrew Johnson said, "This is a country for white men, and by God, as long as I am President; it shall be a government for white men."

Abraham Lincoln said "I will say, then, that I am not, nor ever have been, in favor of bringing about in any way the social and political equality of the white and black races [applause]: that I am not, nor ever have been, in favor of making voters or jurors of negroes, nor of qualifying them to hold office, nor to intermarry with white people; and I will say in addition to this that there is a physical difference between the white and black races which I believe will for ever forbid the two races living together on terms of social and political equality. And inasmuch as they cannot so live, while they do remain together there must be the position of superior and inferior and I as much as any other man am in favor of having the superior position assigned to the white race."

"If I could save the Union without freeing any slave I would do it".
Abe Lincoln to Horace Greeley

George Washington the country's first President was also the owner of over 216 slaves.

Thomas Jefferson was also the owner of more than 187 slaves.

The countries first 18 Presidents either owned slaves while they were in or out of office; the last to own slaves was Ulysses S. Grant.

The President is called the voice of the people, and the leader of the free democratic society, they represented the will of the people. It was therefore the will of the people that blacks be slaves.

America the Brutal

In spite of Americans being told and wanting to believe that this country is the land of the free, and that it is the best place in the world to live, it came at what cost? These personal pursuits cleverly sought to hide an uglier and darker side of its history; this being only one of many. Slavery, however, is one of its most brutal; often celebrated in its day by hundreds even thousands of white Americans.

Here is a history that America would rather forget than to admit its hands were red with the blood of its African American people. White America would rather forget or even deny these things ever took place than to believe they are the most violent people on the planet, many dressed up in the clothes of pretentiousness and racism.

Life for black people progressively worsened over the years. It was the intentions of whites for blacks never to be granted, civil or human rights. Their objective was clear, and that was to have them as property forever.

After hundreds of years of oppression, slaving for masters and suffering horrifically at their hands, one would think the abuse would subside, that the love of God would overrule such practices, but it did not. God had nothing to with the things that took place in the name of their religion.

The violence done to black people brought pleasure even joy to those who inflicted it. It was often celebrated by taking photos, even sending them to friends and loved ones as souvenir postcards.

One of America's most violent histories towards one race of people has almost exclusively been towards black people.

How do you kill a black man? Whip him, castrate him, shoot him more than 200 times and hang him from a tree, go home and have dinner.

A white woman named Lucy Fryer was murdered in Robinson, seven miles from Waco. Jesse Washington, a laborer on her farm (17 years old and mentally retarded), confessed to the murder. In a brief trial on May 15, the prosecution presented a murder weapon and Washington's confession (it was believed that he didn't understand what he was confessing to). The jury deliberated for four minutes, and the guilty verdict was read to shouts of, "Get that Nigger"!

Washington was beaten and dragged to the suspension bridge spanning the Brazos River. Thousands roared, "Burn him!" Bonfire preparations were already under way in the public square. That was where Washington was beaten with shovels and bricks.

Fifteen thousand men, women, and children packed the square. They climbed up poles and onto the tops of cars, hung from windows, and sat on each other's shoulders, looking for a good spot. Children were lifted by their parents into the air. Washington was castrated, and his ears were cut off, all in full view of everyone.

A tree supported the iron chain that lifted him above the fire of boxes and sticks. Wailing in pain, he attempted to climb the hot chain.

For this the men cut off his fingers. The executioners repeatedly lowered the boy into the flames and hoisted him out again. With each repetition, the crowd shouted in approval.

After the hanging, Jesse's body was placed in a burlap bag and dragged around the City Hall Plaza; through the main streets of Waco, finally ending seven miles later at Robinson, where the murder supposedly took place and where a large black population lived. Jesse's charred body was hung for public display in front of a blacksmith's shop.

Six black circus workers were alleged to have assaulted a young white girl on the circus grounds. They were dragged from their cells in Duluth, Minnesota by a mob of about five thousand people.

Twelve policemen were injured during the attack on the jail. In an impromptu trial, orchestrated by the mob leaders, three of the suspects were "found not guilty." Three were "found guilty". Those found guilty were hanged. A later investigation by the civil authorities proved that none of the murdered men could have participated in the assault. The findings, however, did nothing to change the result, so therefore, innocent men died.

Hanging was a death done under the law. This was not so with lynching, as seen in the above. It was a spectacle, an exhibition, guided by violence. There were more people going to a lynching than to church.

Lynching black people was popular, particularly after the abolition of slavery. After the civil war ended and during the reconstruction period of 1865, blacks were given their freedom, but would only be lower class citizens having no civil rights or voting rights. White America was not willing to lose their cash cows, even convincing themselves that slavery was necessary, even just.

Whites would not give up so easily. There had to be a way to keep blacks under their control. Black Codes would be one of the solutions. Every former slave state adopted the Black Codes as a way to further control black people, a restricted freedom; it would be slavery without chains, a prison without walls. These Black Codes would be in effect until 1866 (realistically they are still being used in various places in the United States).

The best way to handle blacks was through violence, since nothing else worked. They did their best to demoralize and dehumanize them. They tried to break their will, kill their resolve, and destroy the black family.

Some of the darkest days in American history followed slavery for black people. After suffering hundreds of years as slaves to be given what they thought would be a new life, finding instead more hatred, segregation, and racism. It was because of this that blacks were disenfranchised, even confused as to why they were still being oppressed. The answers to this and other questions would be found at the end of a rope, and terror in their communities.

In the latter part of the 19th century, it was all too common, particularly in the southern states, to lynch black people. This was an accepted method used by white people to terrorize what whites considered lower life.

Whites hated black people, even feared them for what they might become or would be able to do. Here is another hurdle of hardships that black people would have to jump through for another 100 years. Blacks would have to contend now with what would be called "lynch laws".

"Lynch Laws" in reality were murders open to the public for individuals who were suspected of a crime. Lynching was mob justice, not requiring a court judgment. Prior to 1882, there are no records kept of lynching, but in that same year, the Chicago Tribune began to keep account of lynchings. Beginning in 1912, the National Association for the Advancement of Colored People (NAACP) kept an independent record of lynchings.

Let us look at a few numbers. Between the years 1882 and 1951, there were 4,730 people lynched in the United States; 3,437 blacks and 1,293 white. The largest number occurred in 1892. Of the 230 persons lynched that year, 161 were black and 69 were white. Although a large number of white people were victims of this crime, the vast majority of those lynched, by the 1890s and after the turn of the century, were black people.

In fact, the pattern of almost exclusive lynching of black people was set during the Reconstruction period. The total number of black lynching victims was more than 2 1/2 times as many as the number of whites put to death by lynching. Blacks were often lynched for no reason at all other than racial prejudice. Ranking high on the list of crimes for which they died was rape. It was a crime of presumption. All that was needed was a woman or a child to say they were raped and someone would die. In fact Southerners said they only lynched Negroes for raping white women or for murder.

As with any race, black people believed in their God given right to protect themselves, but white laws prevented them from legally owning firearms, making it easy for whites to take advantage of them. In the years following World War I, a pattern of racial violence began to emerge in which white mob assaults were directed at times against entire Black communities.

Race riots were the product of white society's desire to maintain its superiority over Blacks, vent their frustrations in times of distress, and attack those least able to defend themselves. Black people were passive considering all that had been done to them, but even they could weary of ill treatment.

In these race riots, white mobs would invade black communities, beat and kill large numbers of blacks and destroy black property.

Blacks fought back and there were many casualties on both sides, though most of the dead were black. One of the most amazing riots in the south occurred in Atlanta, Georgia in September 1906. The city for months had been stirred into a fury of race hatred by a movement to disfranchise Blacks.

Twelve rapes of white women were reported in one week, giving the impression that there was a plague of black rape; this was enough for whites to take action. This touched off a riot. White mobs, meeting ineffective resistance by city police, murdered blacks, vandalized and destroyed their homes and businesses. Blacks tried to resist, but found themselves outnumbered and of course outgunned. Some blacks were arrested for arming themselves in self-defense. When the four days of unrest ended, 10 Blacks and 2 whites had died. Hundreds were injured, and over a thousand blacks fled the city.

Why did they leave the city? Loved ones were lynched for attempting to protect themselves. It was violence against whites, and this was punishable by death.

Listed here are a few other reasons why blacks would be lynched:

robbery and theft,

for an insult to a white person,

for various trivial offenses or no offense at all,

disputing with a white man,

attempting to register to vote,

unpopularity,

self-defense,

testifying against a white man,

asking for a white woman's hand in marriage,

for "peeping in a window.

Those charged with crimes such as these did not mean that the person was guilty of that crime. Victims were often known to have been innocent of misdeeds but they were just Negroes.

A special study was done on hundreds of lynchings. The conclusion was that 1/3 of the victims were falsely accused. Frequently whites were mistaken in the identity of their victims, but that did not matter. There would still be a lynching regardless of the facts.

The greatest defense of white people to justify lynching black people was rape. The claim was that black men had an uncontrollable desire and fixation to rape white women (facts however showed that more whites raped blacks than the other way around). It was felonious assault and homicides that triggered the majority of these mob actions.

It was also wrong in the eyes of whites for blacks to defend themselves (a right everyman had the right to do under the Constitution). In order for the mob to have its way, it was better to cry rape which would justify their swift course of illegal action.

By white definition, rape was all sexual contact between black men and white women (consensual or not). Rape was seen by whites as even the slightest physical contact with a white woman or girl.

Often it would be found that many of the blacks that were being lynched would be owners of land that whites desired. Setting them up would ensure they would get that land at the death of its owner. Was this legal? It did not have to be.

The people who made up these mobs were usually small land holders themselves, tenant farmers and common laborers, whose economic condition was very similar to that of blacks. These whites frequently found black men were their economic competitors and bitterly resented any black progress among them.

Because of economical hard times caused by this competition, it was easy to get a mob together for many of these bogus crimes. When the call went out people came. It became an amusement park atmosphere and in some cases there were 5 cent tickets bought by those seeking a good seat for the lynching. They were often community affairs. In attendance were found judges, lawyers and police officers.

We can only imagine what was in the minds of men, women or children, knowing that they were innocent, knowing they were going to die and not one police officer would lift a hand to prevent it. As a matter of fact, between 1882 and 1927 there were 76 black women lynched.

White people feared that blacks were "getting out of their place" since they were no longer slaves and the white man's social status was now being threatened and in need of safeguarding.

Lynching was seen as one of the best methods to defend white supremacy and keep blacks from becoming "uppity". Lynching was more an expression of white Americans' fear of blacks making social and economic advancement than black so called crimes.

W. E. B. DuBois was quoted as saying: "...the white South feared more than Negro dishonesty, ignorance and incompetency, Negro honesty, knowledge, and efficiency."

White people's greatest fear of blacks has been them knowing how to adapt and overcome. To bully them only strengthened their resolve. America has not changed its brutal ways.

It is a known fact that, that which cannot be controlled is feared; that which cannot be contained must be destroyed, if not physically, economically and socially. It is after all the American way.

America's brutal hand reached across the sea into Africa snatching its people away to build a nation that is red with the blood of innocent people who did no more than be born in black skin.

NOTES

Black Owned

Whenever a business grows, it becomes necessary to increase employment to add value and compete with other businesses creating wealth. In the early days of American history, it was tobacco, sugar, rice and cotton that were the main stables.

Plantations could be found almost everywhere. Large or small the one thing they all had in common was slave labor.

Plantations needed workers to work the fields; the cheapest labor there were slaves. Slaves were also a sign of status especially among the wealthy. What would life be without slaves? What would people think? The more slaves the greater the status. Slaves did not have to be paid.

Slavery was big business in more than one way. First, slavery was a way for white America to have someone labor for them at no cost (or very little cost to themselves.) Slaves did the work they were unwilling to do and slaves were the ownership of human beings as property.

Even today we are still confronted with slave labor. When someone is paid what is called minimum wage it amounts to slave labor when you compare to the cost of living. Blacks are still expected to work harder and longer under the scrutiny of modern day taskmasters. Many Blacks in the 21st century are still trying to win the approval of white America by pleasing the master for a check.

There is a bit of history we must take a fresh look at. Just as there are white owned and operated businesses today, the same held true in the past. Whites could have slaves as well as indentured servants. An indentured servant was a white (or black) person who volunteered to work for payment usually meals and a place to stay, during the time of their servitude.

It was stated before that whites owned businesses and slaves, yet there were some blacks who also owned slaves. Yes it is true, blacks actually owned other blacks in the time of slavery in America. How could this be?

How could it be possible that blacks could own other blacks? Is there any proof? Blacks came to America as indentured servants not slaves who were able to earn (buy) their freedom by working off their debt. Those who did were given land and headrights that they could develop often through sharecropping or direct ownership. As a result consider the following:

An 1830 census done in America (we don't know how actuate) showed that there were some 3,775 freed blacks that owned 12,740 total slaves. In Louisiana there were 965 free slaves that owned 4,206. The state of South Carolina showed 464 free blacks owning 2,715 slaves.

It should be noted that free Black slave owners lived in states such as New York and as far south as Florida, westward into Kentucky, Mississippi, Louisiana, and Missouri.

According to that same census of 1830, free blacks owned more than 10,000 slaves in Louisiana, Maryland, South Carolina, and Virginia. The majority of black slave owners lived in Louisiana and planted sugar cane.

The largest black slave owner in the south was a man John Caruthers

Stanly of North Carolina having 163 slaves. The average slave owners had from one to five slaves, but there were at least 6 blacks in Louisiana that owned 65 or more slaves.

The largest number 152 slaves were owned by a widow C. Richards with her son P.C Richards, who owned a large sugar cane plantation. Antoine Duduclet was another black sugar planter with 100 slaves, whose estate was valued at (in1830) $264,000.

Let us be clear on this, because it was not just the wealthy that owned slaves. Besides them there were many people who owned slaves like they owned dogs, cats or any other animal. Many land owners would pay the price of a slave through bartering or even trading livestock. So to suggest that only rich people owned slaves is untrue.

Even during the turbulent time of slavery, blacks were hopeful that there might be a chance for them to be treated as equals to have economical freedom, but there was more to this aspect of blacks owning blacks.

No matter how successful an African American would become, there were still limits put on them and one such limit concerned slavery itself.

There was a statute enacted stating the following;

"No black or Indian though baptized and enjoy their own freedom, shall be capable of any purchase of Christians (meaning any white person), yet not debarred from buying any of their own nation".

So, it was possible for a black to own another black person, but it was not acceptable for any black to own a white person under any condition. A small land owner who is white can own a slave, but a large land owner who is black could not have someone who is white.

It must also be said that every black person who was a slave did not seek freedom. Some have said, this was not true, what human beings would seek to remain in a condition of brutality, inhumane treatment and torture?

Though many slaves were content with their lifestyle, they were not being mistreated or abused. They were fed, clothed, and sheltered.

They had to be ever mindful of the need to comply with the master, because he or anyone in his household could inflict cruel and harsh pain on them for any reason at all. The life some of them led was better than the life they left behind in Africa, but there was fear and no freedom. For some there was food and family.

There were even blacks who were willing to take up arms against other blacks to keep things the way they were.

Blacks heard how black plantation owners were treating blacks on their plantations and would rather take their chances with another white owner.

Blacks began to resent other blacks going back to the days of being brought over on the slave ships. The overseers would place a slave over other slaves during the night watch (as the slaves outnumbered the whites). Slaves were given whips and instructed to use them against other slaves who would speak or get out of hand during the night (the reward for this would often be more food, a shirt and some pants).

Blacks were being taught to turn against their own people. It was brainwashing at its best, and whites were effectively redirecting hate from themselves to other blacks. The war would not only be North versus South, Bond versus Free, Black versus White, but also Black versus Black.

NOTES

Born Disadvantaged

Who are the people we called black, Negroes, colored, or of African decent (American)? Where did they come from and why do they carry themselves as if something is owed to them by the rest of the world?

We will be looking at the history of the black man and his family in America. We need to see if there are any noticeable differences between them and other races apart from the obvious color issues.

For anyone to say that there is no difference, knows little or nothing about what it means to be black, living or growing up in America.

Of course every race can speak of the hardships many of them were confronted with as they began to grow and develop in America. Certainly, all races have experienced hardships and suffering.

Under other circumstances, such a statement would weigh heavy, but no other race of people is still being oppressed, suppressed and repressed like black people in America (this suffering of blacks continue to this day in other countries).

Even illegal aliens coming into this country are given opportunities black people were never afforded. Hispanics have grown in acceptance so much that America has even made Spanish the nations second language. Why not Swahili as our second language? I am only saying what many black people have thought.

Being born other than black has never been a disadvantage. This is why so many blacks have tried to live their lives assuming the looks and manners of others races. Many blacks have no identity other than the one given to them. This was identity theft on the largest scale.

Part of the reason for this is that every other race could assimilate, transition, or blend in. This is not the case with blacks. There is a penalty for not conforming, for not fitting or blending in.

Even to this day blacks are still fighting even among us as to our own identity. We have been labeled with Negroes, black Africans, African Americans, colored, jigaboos, niggers, tar babies, spooks, monkeys, and the list goes on.

Think for a moment back to World War II. It was a time of great fear when the Japanese bombed Pearl Harbor. America worried about its own Japanese Americans who were also naturalized citizens. Why? It could be that some of the Japanese living in America would be sympathizers with the people of their origin.

What did America do? President Roosevelt authorized what was called executive order 9066. It gave the military power to set up military exclusion zones and to legally place its Japanese citizens into internment camps for fear that some of them might become the enemy among us. They were kept in these camps until the end of the war.

Was this unfair treatment for citizens of America? The Japanese believed so and would fight for years for reparations. The United States reviewed their claims and found it wrong to have treated its Japanese Americans so cruelly, and not only apologized to them but granted their families financial reparations as well.

What was the difference between Japanese Americans treatment during that war and the treatment Black Americans received during that war, the wars prior to WWII and since?

The difference is simple since the Japanese were considered **American** and blacks were not. More importantly, the Japanese had human and civil rights where blacks had neither. We will also speak more of this later.

America was called the world's melting pot, where people of all ethnicities and races could come. Where all people could build a life for themselves and their families, find jobs, grow and become wealthy. America is the place where all could live out the creed "all men are created and born with certain inalienable rights", and that "all men are created equal"; all but blacks.

What does it really mean to be black in America? Why are blacks treated much worse than any other race? Are blacks born disadvantaged? I say yes.

White America has spoken saying, "No." Black people have the same rights and privileges as everyone else. Many blacks who have blended in have agreed with whites.

Just because we have been allowed to have certain things, go different places or even speak a certain way does not mean we have been accepted. What it does show is control.

Black people are still doing the Stepin and Fetchit, and Amos and Andy shows. Just look at many of the concerts put on by our people and what they promote.

Many blacks think that having money (lots of it) would solve the race issue. Although they will not admit it, they have found that they are just better off than other blacks. The world of white still sees them as only "niggas with money."

Because we are treated better does not mean we are treated equal. How many of those with money are reaching back and helping other black people? Has the treatment of black people changed because of their actions? Is action being taken to educate or alienate?

One of the greatest harms facing us as blacks today seems to be our fear of knowledge that comes from learning the truth. Because of this dread, we remain disadvantaged as well as disenfranchised.

What began as the problem of birth has quickly developed into a matter of worth. We should not become bitter because of these moments of clarity, but take them and make them an opportunity to shine. We are one of the strongest nations of people on the planet.

There is of course a fear that accompanies our European brothers thinking, and has done so ever since black people have began to rise in recognition. What is that fear?

There is a fear that black people will one day do to white people what they did to them for hundreds of years. Is their fear unfounded? Do they have anything to be concerned about?

There are those who spout that blacks were not and have never been disadvantaged. They have been given more than their fair share. There are poor Hispanics and poor whites as well, so why are blacks seeking attention for themselves?

As Blacks, we are not seeking nor do we want attention, none of which would be necessary if life was unprejudiced. What we do want and expect is equal treatment, equal opportunities, equal pay, and equal rights. These things have not become a reality, but things that other races did not have to fight for, we continue to struggle over.

As of yet, we cannot choose what family we are born into (scientist are working feverishly to change that), and we did not choose what color to be born. Black has become the worlds rejects. Anyone born black in color is the enemy. They should have no rights, and no privileges. Anyone born black cannot be godly, have Christian principles or be saved.

Now, blacks have seen that it is a disadvantage to being born black. Many blacks have opted to no longer be considered black. Some of them have done things to alter their appearance and features to look more European.

So being born black is to be seen by the European world as lower than or subservient to white people, an inferior race according to the book," The Bell Curve."

Blacks have inferior mental acuity (yet the greatest inventions have come from the hands and minds of black people). Every door blacks were allowed to walk through has given opportunity for tremendous strides and advancements from sports to medicine.

Maybe it is not working. Blacks have decided not to let the brain washing take hold. They refuse to let it continue.

The disadvantage that black people are faced with is the one placed on them by society. The disadvantage is prejudice and racist towards its own African American imported citizens. Blacks are equal to every other race on the planet, having as much to contribute as any other nationality.

In order for blacks to prosper on the same level as whites, the playing field must be made and kept level. Treatment must be equal and justice fair to all.

NOTES

Genesis

Everything has a starting point, a place and time of origin, a Genesis. Although we will be taking a look at slavery, it would be impossible to exhaust all the records, documents or accounts found concerning it. That is not the goal here. What I would like to do, however, is shed a little light on the process and progress of slavery from its beginning.

For instance where did slavery come from? We will look at some biblical accounts of slavery dating back thousands of years, to the more brutal time of slavery against a particular race of people (just as man has made advancements in creating tools for good, so did his imagination when it came to hurt, killing and destroying the lives of those who didn't agree with him).

The enslaving of other human beings was nothing new. It has been going on for quite sometime. As with most things, it grew to be accepted as a natural part of man's livelihood. Of course that did not make it right, but the path to man's pleasure demanded freedom from manual work.

This is where things start to take a turn for the worse. When Adam sinned (*sin can be replaced with rebellion if that will make you comfortable, or don't believe in sin*).

Adam was told by God "because you have hearkened to the voice of your wife, and has eaten of the tree of which I commanded you, saying, thou shall not eat of it, cursed is the ground for your sake, in sorrow you shall eat of it all the days of your life; Thorns and thistles shall it bring forth to you; and you shall eat the herb of the field; in the sweat of your face shall you eat bread, 'til you return unto the ground; for out it you were taken: for dust you are, and unto dust you will return." (Genesis.3: 17-19).

Adam was made a slave, to the land, not the slave of another man. But it is man's desire to be a god (he can never be like God in his sinful state; that comes through being born again).

What drives a man to do heartless and evil things against other men? Is it his lust for dominance? Man was given power and dominion over the animal world (***Genesis.1: 26-28***).

Man, however, has never been satisfied with what God has given him and is driven by his own wickedness to be God. In order to accomplish that, he must enslave other men; others must serve under his feet (control).

Man's wicked heart not only seeks to subdue lower life forms or the land, but to rule other men as well. These things are the by products of his rebellious nature.

In simple terms, love frees and wickedness enslaves. In order for wickedness to continue, it must be justified, made or declared right. It has been said, "Where there's a will (desire) there's a way".

Anything can be justified as long as there are enough people to go along with it, including those opposed to the Word of God.

Since man in his present state cannot get along with other men, God had to give him laws to help him govern himself. Man being who he is, oftentimes seek to play God, and once again over steps his boundaries. So man began to make up his own laws, doing whatever he felt led to do. This is addressed furthermore in the book.

Interpretation has led to misrepresentation of revealed truths. It is possible to see whatever we want to see, and wrap ones faith around it. Interpretation will make them happy or at the very least justified in their own mind.

With thousands of years of historical corruption at his disposal, man has only gotten progressively worse. Instead of learning from the past, he has sought to repeat it; the only difference is that over the centuries, he has added new techniques of pain and torture to his brazen acts of evil against other human beings.

As we look back at the last four to five hundred years, we will see one of the most painful times in American history; slavery. It was as much about breaking of the will of African Americans as anything else that was done at that time. Slavery stretched back thousands of years, but the effects are felt just as strong today.

As we look at beginnings, we must examine the history of slavery. It is important that we go back to its source. What or who was the reason for this institution being introduced in America?

There are three names that we must get familiar with as it pertains to slavery, the names, Anthony (Antonio) Johnson, John Casor, and Robert Parker.

Who were these men and what did they have to do with slavery? It is important that we go to the beginnings as we deal with this matter of human servitude.

As black people were already slaves, in other parts of the world its popularity was ever growing. In the year 1619, through the place Jamestown Virginia, slavery finally made its way to America.

The first black people to be imported to America numbered 20. Among them was an African named Antonio or Anthony as he was also called. He was not what was typically called a slave as we know it today. He stands out because of what would later come about.

This first influx of Africans came to the New World as indentured servants to the white colonist, who after working for a specific number of years, could pay for their freedom. During this time of servitude, they learned the ways and business practices of the Europeans (colonist). After gaining their freedom, they were given some land they could develop.

The new freedman Anthony worked off his debt (money for passage to America) in four years and he and his wife (Mary) became landowners.

He was an intelligent African American who built a lifestyle and some wealth for himself. Anthony acquired more land and by the year 1651 sponsored 5 individuals passage from Africans to the new world to work his land, which now had an increase of about 250 acres.

The same principles that applied to Anthony and the first Africans to come to the Americas from Africa, would apply to others as they took this journey to America. At least that is what they thought.

A dispute broke out between Anthony now carrying the last name Johnson (it was common for slaves to take on or be given their owners last names). This dispute with one of his servants, in the person of John Casor (possible Caesar), was concerning his rights.

This conflict was over John Casors' right to freedom. According to Anthony, he purchased John as his servant (slave) for life. On the other hand, John believed it was only for an allotted time. John's words fell on deaf ears with Anthony. John ran away from his plantation to Robert Parkers, hoping to become his servant to work off his remaining time of servitude to gain his freedom.

The owner of the other plantation was Robert Parker a white man. If you have not figured it out yet, the disagreement was between two men of African descent. This argument did not end there. John desired to work off the last years of his servitude on the plantation of Robert Parker.

Anthony was not having it. He took an action that would change the face of servitude for blacks forever. Anthony took the matter to court and had wealth enough to afford it. After a year and a half of battling in court, a decision had been reached, concerning this matter.

In 1654, Anthony Johnson went to court and fought Robert Parker over his right to have John Casor, returned to him, to remain his servant forever.

The court's decision was rendered;

"seriously consideringe and maturely weighing the premisses, doe fynde that the saide Mr. Robert Parker most unjustly keepeth the said Negro from Anthony Johnson his master....It is therefore the Judgement of the Court and ordered That the said John Casor Negro forthwith returne unto the service of the

said master Anthony Johnson, And that Mr. Robert Parker make payment of all charges in the suit.".

With the stroke of a pen, life for black people had changed. They would no longer be considered an indentured servant who could earn their freedom, or be granted land and headrights. What took place had effectively ended all avenues of freedom for those of African heritage. A new institution and a new era had begun for American Africans as they were imported as property slaves.

Anthony Johnson, who had substantial wealth, was still a black man. He was subject to find himself back in servitude by the same law that he helped (even if unwittingly) pass.

Due to many of these fears, he sold his land and moved his family to Maryland, where he rented new land. Look at what took place after his death in 1669. After his death, a jury of white men declared that because Johnson was a negroe and therefore an alien (not a citizen by their standards), the 50 acres of land he had deeded to his son (Richard) in Virginia was awarded to a white man. Anthony Johnson was the wealthiest freed slave ever until the end of the Civil War some 200 years later.

NOTES

Holocaust
(Black Genocide)

The Swahili word for Holocaust is Maafa, this word is familiar to us. It has ringed in the ears of America from WW II and the treatment of Jews by the Germans. Little to nothing is said about the holocaust that plagued black people by the heartlessness of white Europeans starving for power through what they called progress.

Why are black people making so much of slavery? They were not the only ones enslaved. Indians were slaves and as a matter of fact white people too. So no big deal, after all they brought it on themselves.

But slavery was a big deal and it affected everyone. Slavery jump started the English colonies when they moved into the states from Britain.

When the English came to what would later be called America they were completely unprepared for what awaited them. The place they established and began to build was a place called Jamestown, Virginia.

The English began to build and work the land. But there was more work than they could handle or had anticipated and what they were accustomed to, with apprenticeship practices. Here is where it was a benefit for white colonist, because even paying them for services rendered after an agreed on length of time.

Programs such as this allowed the English to pay as their people learned a skill or trade for those who placed their lives on hold becoming servants. Of course that meant leaving their homes and living with those whom they were in service to. This servitude would run between 4 and 7 years.

Whites tired of this type of servitude quickly, so what were colonist going to do? The whites tried another race of people, the Natives (Indians), as they were not called Americans nor are they often referred to as such even now. The labor was too much and difficult for them to bear. Sickness and disease overcame them and many died. Others just run away and the land hid them. Now what would whites do after failure upon failure?

Black people were perfect, their skin color alone would make it impossible to escape or fit into the white culture. The same offer would apply to them as with other races, but would not last long. Later the work practice of apprenticeship would change to indentured servitude, and finally to slavery, loss of all freedom for black people.

Slavery hurt black people the most, whereas, whites enjoyed freedoms and liberties. Blacks cringed because of the pains it brought. Black people suffered such hurt, grief, hardship and mental abuse at the hands of their white oppressors that even history cannot tell of its full impact.

As history unfolds, the numbers detail the hardships and the unthinkable cruelty placed on black people. What was done to them by way of slavery was a death sentence. The Black Holocaust begins to emerge, and was this an attempt to erase an entire race of people? If white people refused to be treated as second class citizens why would they think any other race of people should accept it? Black people were not given a choice.

There were some blacks who gained their freedom, who began their life in America as indentured servants. This would not however last very long as it was determined that the best slaves were people of color. Slavery was as much about color as it was about profit.

Was the purpose of white America to destroy all black people as was the goal of Hitler to rid the world of all Jews? It did not begin that way, and as with all evil actions, the best way to get what you want is to ease it in being very subtle in the approach. Before long others would join in. Fear, became the driving force behind white people's actions towards blacks.

Let us take a closer look at this fear in action. When the first blacks came to this country they did so as indentured servants not freedmen. Their hopes and aspirations were not that they would remain so, but lived believing they would one day be free.

How sad African Americans could not begin life equal in creation to their fellow man. A civil court action would change how black people would be treated for hundreds of years. (Note: Although slavery was new to America it was already flourishing in other countries before 1619.)

Blacks were not afforded human rights or civil rights. They would be seen as property, having no choice in life or death, and because this was true, whites took full advantage of it. This can be seen in their inhumane and cruel punishment of all blacks including those who had won their freedom. It was said **"to shoot a black person was no more than shooting a pumpkin, after all they are no more than property and not human beings"**.

As America grew, so did its need for laborers. In their frame of mind, Africa was a brimming resource filled with savages that could be trained to do the bidding of the white English settlers colonizing the Americas.

Now let us look at the numbers. In 1619, the first blacks were transported to America. They numbered about 20-25. The numbers varied depending on the source. Thirty five years later by 1654, there were over 300 Africans residing in Jamestown Virginias population of 30,000.

Between the years 1540 and 1850, an estimated 15 million Africans were transported to America as slaves.

These numbers do not reflect the number of slaves that died along the way.

This documenting of cargo was not some arbitrary number that was made up by black people. The records were kept by white people to ensure their interest in the property they had purchased. Be aware that the slaves we are speaking about only deal with those that made it to America, not all the slaves that were sold around the world.

There were ships built to carry 400 slaves instead taking more than 800. The slaves were packed so tightly at times they would have to squat and sometimes lay flat as other slave were placed over them.

Chained together by their hands and feet, the slaves had little room to move. It has been estimated that only about half of the slaves taken from Africa became effective workers in the Americas. Many slaves died on the journey from diseases such as smallpox and dysentery and other diseases. Some committed suicide by jumping overboard, while others refused to eat.

The stench was said to be overpowering. During the journey, in bad weather the vents would be closed and breathing would become unbearable. Many slaves became seasick and would lay in vomit and human waste. Some diseases caused bleeding from the rectum and the culmination of this was to lie in.

The following quote is from Thomas Phillips a slave ship captain, from his writing "A Journal of a Voyage" in 1746.

"I have been informed that some commanders have cut off the legs or arms of the most willful slaves, to terrify the rest, for they believe that, if they lose a member, they cannot return home again: I was advised by some of my officers to do the same, but I could not be persuaded to entertain the least thought of it, much less to put in practice such barbarity and cruelty to poor creatures who, excepting their want of Christianity and true religion (their misfortune more than fault), are as much the works of God's hands, and no doubt as dear to him as ourselves."

Many of the slaves were crippled for life as a consequence of the way they were chained up on the ship. Shackles would cut into their skin causing open sores that would be infected with maggots and other diseases. Because they could not bring a profit to the slave traders, they were murdered. A slave could be purchased in Africa for around $25.00 dollars and be sold in America for $150.00 dollars. Slave trading was big business and profits would increase as time goes on.

If 15 million slaves seems impossible, just imagine that is not half the picture. This number represents black people who made it to America between the dates stated. It says nothing of the treatment they received upon arriving.

15 million blacks were thrown into Americas concentration camps, given just enough to remain alive, being treated worse than animals. Forced to work from sun up to sundown every day of the week and in all conditions. If one died they simply replaced them.

Consider the Trans-Atlantic slave trade. Alone, it resulted in the most loss of life for African captives in or out of America. It has been said that over 8 million Africans were killed during their transport and initial landing in America.

It must also be said that the accounting of these deaths may very well exceed the amount actually recorded as shipped. With that note, the amount of deaths would be between 15-50 million, a true holocaust of epic proportions.

Where is the outcry among black people; for the world to remember what was done to them as a race of people who was forced to a land they did not choose?

In 2001 there was a World Conference Against Racism held in Durban South Africa. They demanded an apology for slavery from the former slave trading countries.

There were some European nations prepared to apologize, but there was opposition to this from the United Kingdom, Spain, Portugal, The Netherlands, and the United States who blocked this effort, why? It has been said that there was a fear of financial compensation for blacks if apologized to. They would want what was promised to them, and yes even owed them.

The shackles of slavery have been removed but the burdens remain. Blacks although given more and allowed the freedom of mobility, are still treated as lower class citizens. They still struggle within a white culture. Whites are crying foul, sighting "Affirmative Action", and reverse discrimination laws are seen as unfair to whites.

When the playing field becomes level, there would be no need for any programs such as these, but only those who are racist and believe the right way is the white way are the ones complaining.

Black people are not asking for anything they do not have a God given right to. Blacks were also created in the image of God, and are equally His children by creation to all other human beings.

Racism is as real today as it was 500 years ago. There are those who believe that blacks should not exist apart from doing their bidding and that slavery was the best thing in the world to control them. Yet there are some who say blacks spend too much time trying to get whites to accept them, and those whites who refuse to get their heads out of the sand of ignorance.

Things will not change until we agree that there is a problem and the problem affects and infects us all. It will never go away, but it will get better once we learn to deal with the elephant that is in the room that everyone chooses to ignore.

NOTES

The Bible and Slavery

What does the bible have to say about slavery? Does it condemn or condone it? The arguments are many as it pertains to this matter. It is impossible to make the attempt to give details for many of them, but the one we will focus on is the one that has had the most effect globally which is the slavery of black people.

For centuries, white people have used various methods to control and overpower people and nations around them. In order to do this, they had to have what they considered a justifiable reason for their course of action. As long as the majority was in agreement, it could and would be often made into law. Does this mean it was right? Not at all! It was just "white."

What better way to sanction an action, than to use the Bible. After all it is the word of God, (the problem was, how can wicked, self-seeking, vial and murderous men understand what is holy?). The Bible became a tool for the wicked, and instead of preaching salvation the message was slavery.

What does the Bible have to say about slavery? It says plenty, but we will be directing our attention to the aspect of blacks and slavery and how the word of God has been twisted to fit the need of evil men in their quest for power and desire to be like God. This takes us all the way back to the Tower of Babel, where man sought to build or make a name for himself by building a tower to heaven. All that came of it was more confusion (**Gen.11:1- 9**).

Man has an unquenchable thirst for power. He craved superiority over not just the beast of the field, but over man himself. Sadly, even those who call themselves Christians have been caught up in the belief that slavery was not a sin. Why did they believe something like this? They were told the scriptures (God) supported it.

The majority of this thinking became popular after blacks were brought to the Americas by settlers. Many called themselves Christian people who were missionaries; people who were suppose to be fulfilling the biblical mandate of bringing all men to the knowledge of Christ as their savior. Instead of bringing them freedom, what blacks would ultimately find was slavery. Was this the actions of a loving God?

Let us make this one thing perfectly clear. The Bible does not make distinctions as far as color and class. In fact, the word of God tells us that God is a spirit and they that worship Him must worship Him in spirit and in truth (**John.4: 24**).

The word of God says nothing about salvation for only a certain race of people. It is God's will that none (no one) perish but all come to repentance (**II Peter.3: 9**).

There are those who said the bible condones slavery, and since Jesus and His Apostles never spoke against it, it was therefore alright. Jesus' mission was of a spiritual nature. He knew that if the hearts of men would change, the conditions of men would change also. Read carefully what Jesus said as He entered His ministry (**St. Lukes.4: 14-19**). Jesus' focus was not on the social, economic, or political realm, a changed heart would change habits, and spiritual change would bring about physical change.

Even with that being said, many interpretations followed, and the one used would be the one best suited to the settlers developing economic needs.

As the settlements grew, laborers would be required. They brought servants with them, but they would not be nearly enough. These servants could earn their freedom after several years of servitude.

One of the issues that faced black people was the notion that blacks did not exist in biblical times. Of course this was one of many lies told to them. Blacks believed that they were taken from their homeland, so that they could have a better life, and although it started out that way, it would not remain so.

Blacks would soon be used to describe a race of people rather than a skin color. Blacks at one time were defined as anyone of darker skin, whether Egyptian, Arab, or Ethiopian.

If we are to believe the one view of some bible scholars, then we must believe that there were not black people in scriptures at all, and again this a lie. Why would any God fearing person teach and even promote this lie? There are some scholars who believe that black people were spoken of in scripture but they are not viewed as anything but cursed and slaves.

There are two scriptures references they resort to. The first is that of Cain. When he killed his brother, it was taught that he was cursed with blackness of skin. The second was after the flood when Ham saw his father's nakedness and told it to his brothers. He was cursed by his father Noah for this deed and the curse again was that of blackness. It is these two scripture references that many scholars used to suggest that blacks would be nothing more but slaves to white people (in their view).

There are still some who taught that black people came from the descendants of Cain who married women who were created before Adam (they were called pre-Adamites, if believed means that black people are not descendant of Adam and therefore cannot be saved and would not be human, there were no such people that existed) and the children of this relationship were beings without a soul, who would be slaves forever (of course this means to white people).

Do these things really matter in the greater scope of life? Absolutely, they must be said to help us see the importance of knowing the true history of America, regarding its black citizenship.

Through Abraham we are told all the nations of the earth would be blessed (**Gen.12:1- 4**). Abraham had servants (most commonly called slaves; in the 17th century and following they were seen as servants, these same people are defined differently now) which was Hagar, an Egyptian (dark skinned) woman and the servant (maid) of Sarah.

As we look back let us remember that there were no Laws (Ten Commandments) to govern the people, but there was the law of conscience, knowing right from wrong, good and evil. It was not unusual for a man to have more than one wife, or to have as many servants as they could afford.

How was slavery defined then and now? Hagar got pregnant by Abraham and had his first son Ishmael. Sarah was looked down on by Hagar because Sarah could not conceive. It caused resentful emotions and Sarah wanted Hagar put out of their camp. Was this action taken because of Hagar's color? No, it had nothing to do with the color of her skin or place of origin, but had everything to do with the two women not being able to get along.

History tells us that Ishmael became the father of the Arab Nation and his son by Sarah. Jacob was the father of the Jewish nation. Does this mean that the Arabs would serve the Jews, or that the Jews were better?

Well a closer look reveals differently (**Gen.16:1- 10**). God promised to bless Ishmael in the same way he does Jacob.

Early colonist pulled from the bible what they wanted. Bible scholars used it to justify one of the most brutal lifestyles imaginable to man, not in the form of indentured servitude where one could earn their freedom, but slaves for life.

We see in scripture how Joseph was sold into bondage (slavery) by his jealous brothers (**Gen.37:13-28**).

Jacob willingly became an indentured servant (slave) for 7 years in order to have the right to marry Rachel whom he loved (**Gen.29: 16-21**). Instead he was deceived and married Leah the oldest sister first. When he had fulfilled the week of festivities for the groom, he was given Leah. He remained and works yet another seven years before leaving. There were no other requirements.

Again, none of these actions had anything to do with what color the individuals were. The very book that was written to release men from their sins has been misinterpreted to enslave human beings for no other reason than they were born in dark skin (black).

NOTES

Tolerance Is Not Acceptance

Let us try to put things into perspective. Tolerance is not the same as acceptance. In simple terms, it means to put up with, because of ones inability to eliminate. There are those in America who sought to have blacks removed from this country, seeing them as unacceptable while desiring to send them back to where they came from. There were just as many African Americans who desired to take them up on their offer, establishing what was called "the Back to Africa Movement."

What has been done is done. There is no going back. We cannot undo what has been done, and running away changes nothing. America had opened its Pandora's Box with slavery that can never be shut again. We cannot help people to understand the plight of black people by trying to run away from what has been done to us.

Fear coupled with a history of resentment told us that the best thing to do is flee from oppression. This was what slavery and abuse had taught us, but it was not black people who caused the circumstances that confronted America or the world in the first place.

America is best known for making a mess of things then blaming others for it. America has raped the land and left it barren, then reached out to other lands desiring to do the same to them as well as its people.

As black people we must acknowledge that this is as much our land now as anyone else. We have earned that right through our descendant's blood, sweat, and unnecessary deaths to be here.

There are whites who do not want to face the ugly side of their history; concerning how they could willingly murder human beings and justify it by saying they were not human to begin with.

It was a sin against humanity. This savagery, this butchering and wholesale slaughtering was done by a culture that had placed itself above everyone else, people who called themselves civilized and Christians. This was the welcome Africans received to white European America.

One of the greatest tools that black people have today is knowledge, a tool seldom used in this time of computer access and availability of information. We must seek with diligence to level life's playing field.

It is time that blacks caught up, by stepping up, this will take time, but we are worth it. We must remember our ancestry and be the noble people we know we are and were created to be.

It is easy to put up with things we like and willing to accept as long as we can control the growth process, such as slavery. If it cannot be harnessed, it breeds fear and contempt.

A fearful culture of people is willing to do vicious and cruel things if so moved to do in order to gain compliance. Since they did not want to get rid of blacks, they could make it as uncomfortable and as unbearable as humanly possible when they are around.

In spite of the times, we live in liberty, freedom, justice and equity. Black people are still treated as lower class citizens. Black people are tolerated to a certain degree. Although blacks have been freed from the shackles of slavery, they still suffer from economic, social, and even corporate slavery.

America has placed a new type of slavery upon blacks. This slavery would now work unceasingly on the mentality of African Americans. America would now make it difficult for them to support themselves or their families.

Jobs, unfair practices in hiring, discrimination, and racism, are the new slavery; the newest power over black people. America tolerates them being here, but it does not have to accept them. We hear whites saying the troubles blacks endure have been brought on themselves because of themselves.

One of the greatest harms that can be inflicted on another human being is to cage them up, physically, mentally, or emotionally. How are black people suppose to feel when they are not permitted certain jobs or paid enough to provide for their families?

When white America did not agree with its own laws, they became gangsters, thugs, booze runners and drug dealers. Where do you suppose blacks got the idea to do so?

What white America has said is blacks should be happy to get anything at all to do. If a white person does not want to take a job, then a black may be offered the job at peanuts for pay. Why would blacks take these jobs? They had to feed families that needed stability as well. No one likes to be given leftovers, but that is just what black people were given.

Whites have said that black people are not family oriented; that they were lazy and only care about themselves. Nothing is further from the truth. As a matter of fact, the people who were truly lazy happen to be white, which was one of their many reasons for slavery.

Whites have some culpability for many of the things that have contributed to the downfall of the black family. They had effectively closed up America to African Americans from the inside, having put them in the cage of racism and segregation, with signs on the cages reading Jim Crow.

When you oppress a people for hundreds of years, it undoubtedly has an effect on them. Black people have endured hundreds of years of brain washing. Was it effective? Absolutely, but not entirely.

White America would have to know and have assurance that it was successful in its ill-treatment of blacks. Can they be controlled without the need of shackles without being put in physical cages any longer? Would they believe what they are told, do as they are told and even turn on their own people?

So far so good, blacks are only tolerated. They know they are not accepted even among their own people and this lack of acceptance is now becoming embedded within them. Conscience fear of the past floods their minds and blacks revert back to the things that took place in their past. Blacks quickly surrender within the cages of their minds, doing just and only what they are told.

Blacks were told they would never be accepted, and that the best they could do would be to acknowledge this and stay in their place. Whites have kept blacks at a disadvantage. Illiteracy was high among black people, unemployment and mental illness (distress brought on because of lopsided treatment) was prevalent.

The harder black people would try to get ahead, the deeper the burdens placed on them became, all because of these cages with no bars.

Racism rules tremendously through the channels of segregation. As whites, they have decided to let blacks live among them (in America), they do not have to let them live near or with them (in suburbs of white exclusivity).

If we let them live where we live and have access to the things we do, the next thing we will have to do is treat them as equals. This would not be acceptable in "the white" standards of practice.

Suddenly, labels are the way to go. Label them, and if these labels are successful, blacks would fight among themselves, becoming self destructive. But how would this be done?

When hiring, do not hire any dark skinned blacks. Get those who are light and fair skinned (they were called "passing" because many of them could pass for being white).

Why was this done? It would send a mix message to blacks just as it was when they were slaves and there was what they called "the house niggas" and the "field niggas". The house niggas were treated better than those who worked in the fields.

Accommodations were better, food and clothing was better, and because of this it was easier for those who lived in the house to betray those who worked in the fields. It became a conflict in color.

There are some who do not believe this was true, that color had nothing to do with the treatment of slaves, and that it was not so.

This did not mean those in the field were any darker or lighter than those in the house, but their treatment was better. The matter of color would come into focus because the white slave masters would take black women and force sex with them (they after all were their property). Children often resulted from these rapes, and slave masters would not want their wives to know what they had done, so they would send the children, sometimes with mothers off to other plantations forcing the further division of families.

These children were obviously not dark as other blacks and some of the masters would have them cared for secretly keeping up with their progress and lives. Slaves were not accepting of this, many believing these light skinned slaves were only spies for the master.

Shades of color even today has been used as an unspoken label by whites to cause the same turmoil among blacks as it did in times past when it came to employment.

Unemployment is high among black people, not because they are unqualified for the positions they apply for. It has been shown that many blacks were just as qualified, if not more qualified than many white applicants for the same jobs. The jobs would go to the white applicant before the black, and often the black was not even a consideration. It was just a matter of complying with laws that were put in place for fair employment practices.

Everywhere you looked during the 1900's and today, you can find places that will not accept black people. There is what was called the "Good O Boy" network, with no blacks allowed.

Blacks will continue to be tolerated as long as they know and keep their place, displaying the Willie Lynch mentality, and there is the superior race (white) and the inferior race (black). Blacks and whites can never be equals in the minds and actions of many.

NOTES

Blacks and White Movies

Racism and bigotry were the new wave of conditions blacks had to contend with once slavery ended. It was not only found in the real world, but it could be seen in movies, watched and celebrated on the big screen. When the advent of movies came about, the continuing story of race had a new media to conquer.

Movies from the very beginning had a profound affect on the masses. It was a way to tell history that was not captured apart from photos, and sometimes it was for telling or retelling of history that had to be questioned. Was the telling for entertainment or was there something else?

As movie viewing began to increase, there were many stories to be told. These stories varied as much as their director, as history has shown us. Movies could influence its audience, on the screen as well as behind the screen to the set.

What part did blacks play in film? As we look back at this emerging media, we must know that it was not easy for blacks in motion pictures. Blacks were used in movies, but only on a limited basis. It was said that the first African American appeared on screen in 1898. It was harmless enough! They were seen as soldiers, and again in Uncle Tom's Cabin in 1903. It was not long after this that blacks would be portrayed in stereotypical ways, as thieves, cowards and preachers.

Of course there were black directors of movies. One most notable was Oscar Micheaux who was the first black director of a sound film "The Exile" in 1931. He directed over 35 films from 1918-1948. Many of his works were seemingly lost over the years, and received very little in the way of financing or theater play.

He was also the owner of Micheaux Picture Corp. from 1919-1948. The problems that existed then, for some filmmakers, still exists today; for many black directors who must take the independent movie route to have their movies seen.

There were also three other Black owned studios; Ebony Picture Corp., (1916-1920) The Lincoln Motion Picture Co. (1916-1921), and Norman Studios

(1920-1928). Of course they were not popular, but it was one way blacks could act without being stereotyped.

Slavery and freedom quickly became one of the major themes of the cinema. One of the most notable films was D.W Griffin's "Birth of a Nation" in 1915. It told the story of the Civil War, the Reconstruction Period and how it affected two families; one in the North and the other in the South. This movie was really about slavery and how blacks had brought this plight on themselves. It was the director's views immortalized on film.

This movie was a tool of propaganda. Sadly, not only did President Woodrow Wilson watch the movie, but he bragged about its accuracy as well. This caused a resurgence of K.K.K membership, even causing riots to break out in the North in 1919. Was this D.W. Griffin's goal all along to promote segregation?

What about the black people in his film? Here is a little fact: when it came to blacks in this movie, D.W. Griffin had white people playing blacks whenever they would come into close proximity to white actresses as he did not want them polluted by blacks, (it was said that there was only one real black actor in that movie). Griffin was not the only director to do this. You can see this same thing in the movie "King Kong" in 1932 where white actors playing the natives in most of the shots.

One of the most well known movies of the era was Al Jolson's 1927 movie "The Jazz Singer" (the first talking movie), in which he appeared black faced. The first black talkie was Melancholy Dame released in 1928. The first black feature film was "Hallelujah" by MGM in 1929. Black face is seen again in the show "Amos and Andy", and the majority of movies made in the 1920's and 30's. Blacks who would be given work would be paid little to nothing for any roles they might have found. One of the few exceptions was Paul Robeson. There was also Hattie McDaniel who won best supporting actress in 1939 for her role in "Gone with the Wind". Was Hattie a great actress or was she what white America saw as the best portrayal of a "mammy"; the way all black people should conduct themselves? Hattie was indeed a great actress, but what white people saw was a docile black woman doing just as she was told and getting a reward for doing so. The Academy Award did nothing to change Hattie's life or career.

In the movie the "Imitation of Life" (1934), Natalie Wood played a girl who was half black (Mulatto). At that time it was called passing (for white). Couldn't they have found a black woman to play the role? Sure they could, but she would have to kiss a white man and this was strictly taboo. Her boyfriend, discovering the truth, became violent towards her for her deception. The movies' strong emphasis was on staying away from mixed relationships or deception.

Bessie Smith, Ethel Waters, Duke Ellington, Cab Calloway, Hattie McDaniels, Paul Robeson, Josephine Baker, Billie Holiday, Lena Horne, Marian Anderson, Ella Fitzgerald, Nina Mae McKinney, Sarah Vaughn, Sidney Poitier, and Harry Belafonte are among the most known early Black performers, actors, actresses, and singers, but they were not the only ones.

Even though they brought in money at the box office, they were still treated with less respect than white performers, not being permitted to come through the front doors of many of the places they performed, but using black entrances in the rear of buildings.

Success would bring financial change, not racial change for blacks. They were simply "niggas with money." In modern times, we find that Hollywood is more tolerant of blacks in film but not really accepting of them. Blacks must get in where they are allowed to fit in.

The roles that were often offered to blacks were very minor roles. Or there were roles that showed blacks as slow talking bugged eyed shaking in their boots cowards, convicts, stable hands and not serious dramatics.

Whites stereotyped blacks to give themselves an advantage over them. It was used to keep the belief system of blacks within certain limits. This projected to whites how they are superior to blacks and to show blacks they can never compete with whites, as blacks could not be educated.

Blacks were not considered serious actors. They were seen as comic relief, and simpletons. Although there were some great dancers like Bill "Bo Jangles" Robinson and the Nicholas Brothers, little is said about their talent in the movies as actors but dancers. White's portrait of black people was one of singing, dancing, smiling, happy, but dimwitted people who needed guidance that only their masters could supply. Blacks were pranksters, and were happiest when they did things to please the "masta" and made him happy.

There is no place this is seen clearer than in what was called "minstrel shows." Minstrel shows were popular between1840-1950. These were stage shows consisting of white people in black face, depicting what they supposed to be life of black slaves on the plantation, and black life in general, through humor, dance and demeaning actions, some of which we have already spoken.

These white actors would travel around the country putting on these acts, which became so successful, until people of all ages began to imitate them, including church members, boy scouts and fraternal organizations, and all of them poked fun at blacks. It should come as no surprise that even blacks began to do minstrel shows, making fun of black people to the delight of white audiences. Minstrels would sing black songs while mispronouncing many of the words, and imitate black people dancing and acting like fools (to them this was black life).

There were many blacks that were great actors receiving little in the way of recognition for their works including Dorothy Dandridge (who in 1954 was the first black nominated for a lead character by the Academy for her role in "Carmen"), Paul Robeson, Ethel Waters, Nina Mae McKinney (billed as the first black love goddess of the screen), Lena Horne, and Carmen Jones (who was a mulatto).

Black people in the movies have made great strides over the years, but the struggle is far from over. Hollywood is allowing blacks to gain some access in the movie industry such as Will Smith, Denzel Washington, Halle Berry, Morgan Freeman, and Danny Glover. These are exceptions, but Hollywood is recycling the same actors. There are many black actors and actresses looking for their big break to get into movies.

As we examine blacks and whites in movies, we must remember that the earlier events of movies took place during the Jim Crow era. Whatever blacks were seen as was based on white America's opinions, perception and imagined fears.

Blacks were considered silly, stupid, ignorant, inferior to whites, and that is what whites would show their world on the movie screen.

Making fun of black people was the norm. It was what white people saw black people as that mattered on film. They had jet black skin, big lips and bulging eyes, speaking slowly because they were not intelligent. Just look at Rochester with Jack Benny. Television is another story all together.

Blacks would play the roles of the fool to white America. It was at least their way of making it into film, to get work and to feed their families. Many blacks suffered the pains of white treatment in films not because they wanted to, but often to just survive and keep food in their homes.

Lincoln Theodore Monroe Andrew Perry, born May 30th, 1902, a name that is not familiar to many of us. He has been in countless movies and seen on TV. He was the first black actor to become a millionaire, having more than 12 cars and employed 16 Chinese as servants, but he lost his fortune and filed bankruptcy in 1947. This man would be known to the world as "Stepin Fetchit" (he took the name from a racehorse he said won him some money).

Stepin Fetchit became one of the black community's worst pictures of the stereotyped black man. He represented everything blacks were not and everything whites wanted to believe they were. As I spend time writing this book, it saddens me to know what my brothers and sisters in times past had to endure. If it had not been for them, you and I could not enjoy the lifestyles we do. What they could not change then, we must not continue to allow today.

Stepin Fetchit once tried to sue CBS for defamation of character for what they said about the character he played. He lost, but in 1976 he received a special Image Award from the NAACP.

The 70's became the time of what would be known as the time of the Blaxploitation films era. All at once it seemed black films were in, (but they still had to say what Hollywood wanted them to say, as it was they who bankrolled the projects, they would also be directed by whites).

Even then, blacks were not shown in the best light. Movies such as "Coffey

Brown", "Shaft", "Blacula"," Cleopatra Jones", "Black Belt Jones", "Sweet Sweetback" put money into the coffers of Hollywood and small change in the actors' pockets.

There were blacks such as Fred Williamson, Pam Grier, Richard Roundtree, and Jim Brown who found work. These movies did not have quality acting. Instead, they focused on violence, sex and foul language; three things whites claim blacks are known for.

These movies having black stars showed the bad guys as white. Millions of tickets sell at the box office just for blacks to get a chance to see the white villains die. This represented the white oppressor getting his reward for all the things he had done to black people through slavery. These movies had the hidden message of revenge, and could be studied to determine the thinking pattern of black people. It was about more than just money.

Were these movies any different from those of the Jim Crow era? Actors needed work, and work brings money. Did they have to act? Probably not, because all they had to do is show the battle between black and white, but this time the blacks were winning and that would fill theaters. Let us remember there is overt racism and there is covert racism. For instance, it has become the new wave in movies to have black people die in some of the more horrific ways on film. They cannot die like the average person. It is often gruesome and to say the least, unnecessary, but then again maybe it is just me.

      The next time you watch a movie, pay attention to how few black people are in it, and then watch to see how much screen time they receive compared to their white counter parts. If it is a horror movie or fantasy movie, observe carefully how the black person usually dies.

Notes

Only the Strong Survived

In the world of slaves and slave traders, it was a matter of the strongest surviving the long sea voyage that would take months and thousands of miles. On board for this journey would be those who were paid to get this special cargo to America. These trips across the globe took place in all kinds of weather conditions.

Not only was the environment hostile, so were the conditions on these ships. Thousands of slaves were stuffed into cramped spaces. Areas that were meant to carry two hundred would instead have more than a thousand. A third to one half of them would die at sea.

There was no honor, no glory, no decent burial to accompany these men and women who were taken from their land and their people. Instead, they were met with just enough to keep them alive during this horrendous ordeal. If they died on the journey they simply became food for the sea.

There was sea sickness, disease from being stacked on top of one another. Some of this human cargo died along the way from eating whatever they could to drinking their own urine. They ate fecal matter, and body parts of those who died before they were thrown overboard. Many of them did whatever they could to survive. The ruthless slave traders also published to others how these slaves were barbaric cannibals and savages for what they did to survive. According to them, no Christian white man would do such a thing.

Let us examine that thought for a moment. The date was October 13, 1972, when a group of 45 people crashed in a plane in the Andes Mountains and found 72 days later. There were only 16 survivors. How did they survive, what kept them alive?

The survivors of that crash did the unthinkable. They resorted to eating the flesh of their dead friends to stay alive. Curiously we heard no outcry saying they were cannibals, barbaric or savages. There have always been two standards; one for white people and another for black people (made up as they needed them and passed into law such as the Fugitive Slave Act).

The slaves that made those awful trips had to endure one hardship after another, from physical to mental abuse, yet it was nothing compared to what was ahead for them. I am sure many of them would have chosen death at sea, had they known what awaited them when they reached dry land.

Blacks immediately became nobodies as far as their captors were concerned. Their name and culture would be no more. They would have no life and no family. They would now be told what to do, when to do it, and they had no choice as to who would live or who would die. In fact they would not be treated as people. They had become property (animals were treated better than blacks were).

We can only imagine the fear they felt as they were dragged from their homes, as they witnessed loved ones being slaughtered when they tried to defend themselves.

Today actions like these would be viewed as crimes against humanity, but then it was all business, that is, the way of life. People were paid for human trafficking. This cargo, although throwaway, would be the most precious of all, a way for Europeans to have their cake and eat it too.

Black people are a strong people. They would have to be in order to resist the evil that was placed upon them by white slave masters and their families. They had been brainwashed to believe they were not human, but animals with no rights.

Slaves had psychological games played on them. Many of them were punished, whipped, beaten and abused for no other reason than to put fear into other slaves. It was nothing to take a slaves baby and kill it in front of the parents to break their will.

How did they do it? How did they survive? They did not know or understand the language. This was no problem for the slave masters, because they would use what they always used to get what they wanted, which is violence.

Bloodshed would be used to control them, to give them physical reminders through pain what would be expected of them, as well as what could happen to them. If they did not comply, it was truly "do or die." Death could come at any moment, having no warning.

Although we have focused on slavery in America, let us not fool ourselves. Slavery was global and very profitable. People from all over the world were participating; the West Indies, Cuba, Barbados, Jamaica, Haiti, South America, France, and Portugal all owned slaves. There were not many countries that were not affected by slave trading. By the year 1768 there were over 10 million slaves in America alone.

Slavery (forced imprisonment), was another victory for the European invaders of another land, another opportunity to force foreign ways on people they considered a godless and heathen society.

NOTES

They're Only Children

What did we do wrong? Why are they treating us this way mama? Why are you crying? Did Mr. Gilmore beat you? How does a parent who is a slave tell their child they are not considered human and must do whatever their master desires?

A Mother's tears would often hide the hurt they had to endure for the safety of their children (black women would not often cry in front of their children as not to appear weak to them when it came to the suffering they had to endure). A drunken white man could come into their home and do whatever he chose to do. When he violated a black woman it was not seen as rape. She was no different than a piece of furniture to her white owner.

She could not protect herself other than mentally. She had to learn to pretend that it would get better and nothing happened. Many black men and women died hoping things would change for them. That day never came for them.

Often black women became sexual objects for their white masters, most unwillingly, and some willingly, in order to protect themselves. They even turned in other blacks who were plotting to revolt against their masters. We must not fault them for their actions. Given the circumstances they were in, they were seeing blacks die all around them family as well as friends.

But the hardest thing for the black family to deal with was the abuse they had to endure against their children. Children were not exempt from white violence or brutality. They were sometimes used to get the adult slaves to comply. Slave masters knew of the love blacks had for their children. It was not uncommon for one plantation to have complete family units. Some masters believed the slaves worked better if kept together.

It became clear that black life would not be easy. I am certain that many mothers prayed not to become pregnant. If they did become pregnant they would pray to lose it or hope for a boy.

Slavery was so profitable that plantations would even breed the strongest blacks hoping to produce an even stronger slave. If they could breed blacks, they would save money because they no longer had to import them. As sad as it may be, black women would rather have male children.

To the plantation owners, a slave was a slave and as long as they did what they were told. The masters appeared to be pleasant even compassionate, until there were questions or disobedience. Slaves would feel the wrath of "Mr. Gilmore."

Children were being bred for domestic and household chores. If they were chosen for household duties, they were often treated better than those who were in the field. They would receive better clothing, food and warmth, yet were treated more like pets than human beings.

They had to be available 24 hours a day everyday at the masters every call. Being in the house had major disadvantages. White slave masters were sadist. When it came to discipline they could be cruel, unforgiving and it mattered little that they were children.

Children who were house servants missed out on the support of the family in slave quarters. They soon opposed blacks in the field, even though they were slaves themselves. They felt (indoctrinated to believe) they were better than those outside the house simply because of the treatment they received. Their family was no longer black, but white. Many children lost their sense of culture with its powerful sense of community. **These things were not done by accident, but by design.**

The enslaving of African Americans was a matter of survival; emotional, psychological, physical, and financial for white America.

Children had to learn how to be "good slaves", "good pets", and docile creatures to do their masters bidding without question.

Black women instilled in their children the need to be two people, one inside, and the other outside. The one inside had to be strong to endure the abuse that was sure to come. Young boys who did not respond quickly to the master or his family would be whipped regardless of his age.

There was no respect for the black family. Slavery was as much about destroying the will of blacks as anything else. Whites wanted blacks to be mindless, and what better way than to do it through children. Unfortunately, white life would be seen as the right life for blacks back then as well as now.

As white people loved their children so did blacks. The greatest fear that black women had for their children was daughters suffering at the hand of heartless sex crazed white plantation owners or their task masters.

A black mother worried for their daughters growing older. They knew white men would be looking at them as they developed and tearfully knew that one day they might be taken advantage of sexually. They hoped that teaching them to be modest would have men respect them.

Today several vial, cruel, and murderous type of people behave like slave owners. Many of them would do whatever they wanted to without fear of reprisal including the murder or rape of little children.

It was bad enough that young women and girls would be raped by whites. In order to dehumanize them, they would also gang rape them, leaving but a shell of the woman she was or could become. Actions such as these served to make the black woman believe she was less than human, and this was the goal all along.

The black woman could never call them the monsters they really were.

She could not tell her side of the story or plead her case. Maybe she brought it on herself, that it was all her fault. No she was a thing, a piece of property. This is still the lie being declared today when a black woman is raped or abused. The faces have changed but the story remains the same.

A slave child's childhood lasted for the first 4 to 5 years of life. During this time life seemed relatively normal, sometimes playing and spending time with other children of the house.

Whites also saw that after a time, slaves were becoming more expensive and their affordability was becoming dangerously high and less cost effective for the plantation owners. There was a cure for this matter. Why purchase slaves when all they had to do is have (force) sex with the black women who would have children.

There was a small problem with this action. How would the child be defined? Would the child be black, white, bond or free? There must be laws put in place that would help whites continue this abuse of black people. In or around 1662, Virginia had a statute which said that a child's race would be determined by the mother (prior to this the child's race was always whatever the fathers race was). Why this change?

It was a business decision plain and simple. This was a way whites could take advantage of black women through pregnancy. If the woman was a slave, the children born to her would also be slaves. What it means is white men could force sex on black women for the sole purpose of getting them pregnant cutting down on the need of purchasing more slaves. They could now breed their own.

It was alright for a white man to take advantage of a black woman having sex with her with no consequences to follow (as far as whippings and later lynching). White men were not so accepting of a white woman having sex with a black man. To do so could often bring about the death of that man.

Women could be put out of the colony forever for indulging in what they considered a forbidden act. This sexual wickedness was not about breeding, but control. Whites could do just about anything to slaves with little or no reprisal.

It was believed that if you wanted a good slave you had to raise "it" yourself. This was one of the main reasons for interracial sex. Bear in mind that the plantation master or his overseers would take advantage of this wicked act against black women as well as their teenage daughters.

The death rate of slaves was extremely high and slave masters forced breeding on their slaves to keep their plantations populated. They would have sex with the slaves (they called them wenches) in order to do so.

Some of these plantation owners went as far as promising many of these women their freedom if they bare at least 15 children. The unfortunate part of this was the slave masters having girls as young as 13 being impregnated baring at least 4 to 5 children by the time she was 20 years old.

America today is now at war against unwed mothers. It has now become less profitable, even shameful for women to have children they cannot care for. Where was the call for help not seen for black women who had no choice but to give in to white slave masters who abused their bodies and stained their souls for life? Slave masters even destroyed these same women's children. It did not matter that they were just children.

NOTES

Black Codes

What are black codes and how did they affect black people? What was their purpose? Black codes came into existence during the time of reconstruction just after slavery was abolished and during the Presidency of Andrew Johnson. In fact under his administration as president in April of 1866 he vetoed a civil rights bill which would have granted blacks freedom from Southern black codes (laws that placed severe restrictions on freed slaves such as prohibiting their right to vote, forbidding them to sit on juries, limiting their right to testify against white men, carrying weapons in public places and working in certain occupations).
    Andrew Johnson speaking to Thomas C. Fletcher the governor of Missouri was quoted as saying; "This is a country for white men, and by God, as long as I am President; it shall be a government for white men." Further his views on racial equality was made known in a letter he wrote to Benjamin B French the commissioner of public buildings stating, "Everyone would, and must admit, that the white race is

superior to the black, and that while we ought to do our best to bring them up to our present level, that, in doing so, we should, at the same time raise our own intellectual status so that the relative position of the two races would be the same."

These black codes forced restrictions on freed slaves such as prohibiting them the right to vote, forbidding them from sitting as jurors, even limiting their right to testify against white men, or carrying weapons in public places and working in certain occupations, all things whites were permitted to do.

Black codes made it illegal for whites to educate black people. If they were caught teaching them to read or write, it was a misdemeanor and they would be fined one or two hundred dollars. If a black person was caught doing the same they would be fined, imprisoned for 30 days or whipped (20 or 30 lashes).

Black codes were to keep blacks from total freedom. It would keep them from enjoying the same life as whites. They wanted blacks to believe that although emancipated, they were not truly free, and with the establishment of black codes, they would mentally and socially be hindered. It limited what they could do, where they could live or even if they could relocate to another state.

Let us take a closer look at some States with black codes. For instance Mississippi's black code stated: Negroes must make annual contracts for their labor in writing. If they should run away from their tasks, they forfeited their wages for the year. Whenever it was required of them, they must present licenses (in a town from the mayor; elsewhere from a member of the board of police of the beat) citing their places of residence and authorizing them to work.

Fugitives from labor were to be arrested and carried back to their employers. Five dollars a head and mileage would be allowed such Negro catchers. It was made a misdemeanor, punishable with fine or imprisonment, to persuade a freedman to leave his employer, or to feed the runaway.

Minors were to be apprenticed; if male, until they were twenty-one, if female, until eighteen years of age. Such corporal punishment, as a father would administer to a child, might be inflicted upon apprentices by their master.

Vagrants were to be fined heavily. If they could not pay the sum, they were to be hired out to service until the claim was satisfied.

Negroes might not carry knives or firearms unless they were licensed. It was an offense, to be punished by a fine of $50 and imprisonment for thirty days, to give or sell intoxicating liquors to a Negro. When Negroes could not pay the fines and costs after legal proceedings, they were to be hired at public outcry by the sheriff to the lowest bidder...."

"In South Carolina persons of color contracting for service were to be known as "servants," and those with whom they contracted, as "masters." On farms, the hours of labor would be from sunrise to sunset daily, except on Sunday. The Negroes were to get out of bed at dawn.

Time lost would be deducted from their wages, as would be the cost of food, nursing, etc. During absence from sickness, absentees on Sunday must return to the plantation by sunset. House servants were to be on call at all hours of the day and night on, every day of the week.

They must be "especially civil and polite to their masters, families and guests." In return they would receive "gentle and kind treatment." Corporal and other punishment was to be administered only upon order of the district judge or other civil magistrate. A vagrant law of some severity was enacted to keep the Negroes from roaming the roads and living the lives of beggars and thieves."

Although free blacks were to still call the people they now work for "master." They still had to work from sun up to sun down to be paid, and as we know there were no real jobs that black people were allowed to hold.

In that same year of 1866, an organization came into being that would keep terror in the hearts of blacks. They had no problem with murdering black people or their families if they believed it would further their cause. They were called the Ku Klux Klan, and wherever violence was found they could also be found. There was no greater need than now; this would be the best tool to keep black people in line.

So the black codes, hand and hand with the K.K.K. seemed to be an unstoppable combination. Black codes became necessary after slavery was abolished because no one knew what to do with all the free blacks. More importantly, what would now happen to white economics? After all it was blacks who was really building the country without any of the benefits or enjoying its blessings.

Blacks were even allowed to attend church but restricted to a certain areas (slave pews). They could listen but not participate, and it was forbidden for them to join or become Christians. To do so would mean they are equal to white people. If they were to preach they would have to obtain permission from whites. Black people were not permitted to have homes within town limits zoned for white people only.

South Carolina established black code laws immediately after the Civil war, a few of them read;

"No person of color shall migrate into and reside in this state, unless, within twenty days after his arrival within the same, he shall enter into a bond with two freeholders as sureties."

"Servants shall not be absent from the premises without the permission of the master" Servants must assist their masters "in the defense of his own person, family, premises, or property." No person of color could become an artisan, mechanic, or shopkeeper unless he obtained a license from the judge of the district court – a license that could cost $100 or more.

Every state had varying versions of black codes; clearly the purpose of these codes can be seen. They only served to bind, hinder and add new restraints to freed black people. It would be burdens they would not carry themselves, yet they had no issue with placing them on black people.

It must also be said, these same black codes would later be changed to a more deceptive name called "Jim Crow Laws".

NOTES

Blacks History

Where did black people come from? Are they real? Do they have tails? Can they be trained to fit it? Can they learn? Are black people just diluted white people?

There is much in the way of conjecture as to where blacks came from and we will examine a few of them. Let us begin by saying that none of us could choose the family we were born into, and certainly none of us chose what color we would be born. Yet color has become a symbol of status and privilege. Being born any color but black gives automatic entitlement to such privileges.

There is a belief that has been passed down from generation to generation which has been commonly accepted in this culture (**this culture I refers to is dominate in the United States**).

There is the right (**white**) way of thinking and the wrong (**other than white**) way of thinking. Every thought must meet white approval. How is this so? Where is the proof?

The proof is all around us. As a black man who has grown up in a white world, taught by a white culture what to believe, how to dress, how to work and play, how to fit into their world if I was to be accepted and honored by them.

This is not terrible in itself (learning cultures), but when we are taught that we have no right to think for ourselves, live our own lives, seek wealth, or worship the way we choose, then there is a problem.

There is white belief and there is black thinking. Here is where blacks have a distinct advantage. We know how white people think, feel and respond to life. As blacks we have been taught the way of "white." If you want to be right, you have to **"do it white"**.

But whites have never been in the position of being black, being repressed or suppressed as they have. They have not been violently uprooted and taken from their homeland and their families sold into slavery, butchered or treated with disdain. (If they had been they could never treat another human being the way blacks were being treated).

The great white way has been the so called guide for humanity. This white way often falsely used religion as its cloak to further that belief and to sanction its action.

    As a black man, I have both seen and experienced this process. As blacks, we are taught that love, happiness, joy and fullness of life is white, that civilized men were white and everyone else were savages and heathens. If they (**non-whites**) could not be disciplined or tamed they should be destroyed.

    People who boast their love for God, and that all men are created equal also promoted the thought in the sixties "white is alright, yellow is mellow, brown hang around, black keep back." This was one of the many versions I've heard. Of course racism predates sayings such as this.

    Why is there such hatred by whites towards blacks? Blacks were not lining up and volunteering to come to America. But it must be said that the establishment of this country was built on the sweat, backs and blood of blacks. So why is this race of people chosen above all others to continuously be persecuted by white Europeans?

    I want to take some time to examine this thought, where blacks came from? Maybe if we knew where they came from it might explain the process of white thoughts and their resistance to them.

You see the common (***white***) belief is that whites are superior to all races (its biblical they say). Wasn't that what Hitler was all about; white supremacy through the Arian race?

Life is not about color, but living life to its fullest. One color is not better than another as far as God is concerned.

What about blacks and other races? Are they only sub cultures, therefore having no real importance or value in this European (***white***) world except as they are positional and conditionally labeled?

Let us take a closer look at the aspect of the introduction of blacks. To do so we will take another look at the Bible. White cultures have used it to support its beliefs. I also believe all life comes from God who is the creator of all things.

I believe also that God created man in his likeness and his image (**Genesis.1: 26**). Herein is where the majority of mankind's problems began. It does not come from reading the scriptures, but the misunderstanding and the misapplication of them through ignorance and personal private interpretation. People often see only what they want to see in order to form their own opinions or belief systems.

Since everything began with creation, we must look at it to see where the teaching went astray. First let us look at the name Adam. In the Hebrew tongue it means "man", which includes woman (**Gen.5: 2**).

Depending on who is doing the interpreting, Adam means "red." Therefore, some scholars take it literally to mean Adam was a red man or coming from near the surface, therefore making him light (white). How this thinking came to be I cannot imagine.

The meaning of a word did not suggest literally. For instance, when the Lord told Abram he would father a child in his old age, his wife Sarai heard this and laughed within herself at the thought. When confronted with what she did she said it did not happen (**Gen.18: 10-15**).

The Lord reprimanded her and told her the child's name would be Isaac, which means "to laugh". Did this mean his color was laughter, or even that he would be laughing all the time? Again not true. Could it have just been the joy she would have knowing she would conceive and have a child in her old age could that have brought about the internal laughter she thought no one could hear?

As we look at these names, I want you to know that names carried with them meanings. Look at Isaiah 7:14, a prophetic verse concerning the Lord's future advent (coming). Here his name is to be called "Immanuel", meaning "God with us". Was this to be taken literally?

Let us turn now to the New Testament and the fulfillment of that scripture. St. Luke. 1: 26-31. Mary was told that the child she would conceive and bare should be called "Jesus", which in Hebrew was Josuha, or Yehweh, translated to mean "the Lord". Did this name represent or literally mean a color? I suppose if you tried hard enough you would come up with anything you want.

These meanings could be and were often misunderstood, more times than not, as they were twisted to fit a reader's polluted perception. As stated before, names carried meanings.

Oftentimes, several and much debate comes from how various people would interpret them. Of course, there are those who will even argue the existence of God. For me to do so would be to argue my own existence -- I am therefore He is.

That being said let us re-examine a few words. After doing so, we will lay them side by side with the word of God and see if there is any correlation that can be seen. As we are looking at the history of black people, we must go to the beginning.

As we have already stated, all life came from one, all of us are descendants of the first man Adam regardless of color. Once Adam had sinned, he and his wife were put out of paradise (Eden) and Eve bare children to him.

It should be noted that throughout the bible the male was often the dominate character (this did not mean that women were of lesser importance), only that man had the responsibility to be the leader and provider. This alone is another book...

At the time of his death, Adam was 930 years old (**Gen.5: 5**) and many children were born through him male and female. The first were Cain and then Abel. It would not be long after this that corrupt man would begin to give his own opinions as to what followed when it came to mankind's pigment.

Cain the older of the two brothers, killed Abel when God did not accept his offering (**Gen.4: 4, 5**). Often the case, jealousy motivated Cain. It ate at him as racism eats at people today. Cain refused to accept what God did and lashed out and murdered his brother (**Gen.4: 8**). Man's anger, though aimed at God, (they cannot see) is taken out on others (they can see).

What was the punishment that resulted from Cain's murderous act? He was cursed only as far the land and his ability to cultivate it (**Gen.4: 11, 12**). Bare in mind that he was a tiller of the land (**Gen.4: 2**), and that this curse would affect his very livelihood. It would be too much according to him to bare (**vss.13**).

There were no Ten Commandments for Cain or anyone else to follow, but they did have the law of conscience, knowing good and evil. Evil must be punished as it was when Adam was driven from the Garden.

What would be Cain's punishment? The very land he cultivated would not produce or yield to him. Is that all?

What would people do once they found out that he had killed his brother? Would they want a murderer among them? Would he do the same to them if he did not get his way? No one would help him. He could die or even be killed because of it.

Cain feared that he would be murdered as he did his brother, so God set a mark upon him (**Gen.4: 15**). From what I understand about the word of God, this was not the only time the Lord used a mark.

The mark referred to here was not a mark **"on"** Cain but a mark **"for"** him. When it concerns signs, it was always clear from God as to what it was, but in the case of Cain there is no clarity. Often, where things are left unclear, many so called scholars attempted to fill in these blanks with their own interpretations. As with Cain, promoting this mark as darkness of skin, justifying slavery, and blacks being servants to others forever. I will speak more of that later.

The issue of color did not mean much historically until after the flood. Not to the principles of that time but, by later day interpreters who sought to use color as issues of justification of deeds. What is it that caused all the color controversy? I only spoke of Cain because there are some who teach that he was the father of the black race, I disagree.

NOTES

Enemy at Home

In times of war, everyone comes together against a common enemy, having a single goal, to defeat those who threaten their livelihood, freedom, and country. People from all walks of life came willing to die to protect their right to life, liberty and the pursuit of happiness.

Man has been at war since the fall in the Garden of Eden. His war has always been an internal conflict taken outside to others by his actions of distrust, even jealousy towards others.

War was about power, superiority, and even suppression. War is one way of bringing people together who think alike (not always for the better), but it could also have the reverse effect as we found when it came to its African American people.

We will look at war at home and abroad, and how it affected blacks as a race of people. It must be said that no matter what black people have been confronted with, they overcame it. They are not only strong but resilient, as we will see here, and because of this, other races of people fear them and want to destroy them, if not physically, emotionally and psychologically.

Blacks have suffered from internal wars since they were taken from their homes in Africa. They were knowledgeable of wars as many of them were sold into slavery being prisoners of Tribal conflicts. Rather than kill them, it became profitable to ship them to the New World; a fate that proved to be worse than death.

It would be wars that forced them to this place called the Americas. Originally the first few Africans came as indentured servants to the colonies, but it would not be long, about 35 years and this would all change.

The role of blacks would change forever. Who they were before coming to America would be no more, at least not for 3 centuries and not without ongoing legal and moral fights.

Because man is vial in his ways and evil in his intentions, it was no strange thing for him to seek godship; a desire to be a supreme being, not just over animal life but human life as well, a lust for power.

Man seeks ultimate control and what better way to exercise it than over other human beings. Black people became the best subjects for this evil.

In blacks continuing fight for acceptance, they would do whatever it took to achieve it. As whites need for control grew, so did his cravings for more as a drug addict seeking a high. Since man cannot get alone with himself, he sought what others had in their possession, and in doing so brought about wars.

A line of division was drawn between the north and south. The north did not believe in slavery whereas the south did. The inevitable happened. War broke out, and blacks saw this as a chance to win their citizenship and white approval.

In a society that called itself democratic, it was not when it came to its black people. War, as unfortunate as it was, might very well be the thing that could redeem black people. From slaveries inception in America in 1619 to its conclusion in 1865 there are 4 major wars that broke out during that time, and we will look briefly at them. The American Revolution (1775-1783), The War of 1812 (1812-1815), The Mexican American War (1846-1848), and The American Civil War (1861-1865).

African Americans served in those wars as well as the following wars, The Indian Campaigns (1866-1890), The Spanish-American War (1898), World War I-European War (1914-1918), World War II-European War (1939-1945), The Korean War (1950-1953), The Vietnam War (1959-1973), and The Persian Gulf War (1990-1991).

Blacks did not seek exemption from any of these wars (they did not cause), but they did seek to be treated equally in and out of the military with the same respect as white soldiers. What African Americans found instead was no matter what they did, they remained the enemy at home.

Unfortunately, many records of African Americans' services in earlier wars have been lost or believed destroyed, but some have been found over the years. African Americans fought side by side with whites. The reason for blacks fighting was two fold: 1) they were helping to fight for independence with whites against British domination, and 2) for critical acceptance and equality from whites.

It was said that the death of Chrispus Attucks was one of the major reasons for the **American Revolutionary War**, which leads to open discussion, but colonist wanted nothing more to do with British rule. During the Revolutionary war, there were more than 5,000 African Americans fighting and struggling also for independence.

The land ran red with the blood of many slaves but in the end they had gained no respect, no love, and no appreciation.

It would be during the Presidency of James Madison, America again would have to do battle with the British, leading to the **War of 1812.** The British was supplying arms to the Native Americans who resented the westward movement of United States territories.

In 1808, two years before the war, slave importing was banned, but that did not stop more than 250,000 slaves from illegally being shipped to America.

In spite of their bondage, blacks were still ready to fight for their country serving in all capacities, on navel vessels in mixed regiments and even all colored regiments.

One commendable unit found in Philadelphia was the 26th infantry consisting of some 247 blacks, giving their support and lives for the freedom of the country. When the war ended on December 24, 1814 some fighting continued until August 6, 1815. Growth brought about change, but not for black people.

During the Presidency of James P. Polk, war was again in the air. This war was the **Mexican American War**, a political war between America and Texas. At its heart was the issue of slavery. Texas was a slave state that wanted to protect its interest and was willing to fight for that right.

Blacks were willing yet again to serve, but many whites did not like the thought of black enlistment. The service of blacks was conditional at best, but they served willingly and unselfishly.

In a country known for war, another loomed on the horizon, a war that would bring more death and destruction to an already unstable nation. It was a conflict between the States that would bring about **The American Civil War,** dividing it, which began in 1861.

Jefferson Davis was now President of these New Confederate States of America. The war that ensued would be a battle of north and south, slavery verses freedom.

This would be the greatest opportunity for African Americans to date. They lived in fear but grasped at hope that one day they would be free. If they served, they fought and gave everything. At least they could have their shackles removed to join the military. There they could get a good meal, and warm clothes to wear; even death would be a welcome release.

It was the promise of freedom that kept them fighting. It was hope against hope, yet no matter what they did acceptance was not forthcoming. By the end of the civil war, roughly 179,000 black men served in the U.S army, another 19,000 plus in the Navy, with more than 40,000 giving their lives.

There were more than 80 black commissioned officers, black women who volunteered as nurses, spies, and scouts, whose bravery is still in large part overlooked or forgotten.

Black people gave their lives for a freedom that would never be theirs to enjoy. Even though they were lied to, they moved forward never breaking ranks or turning back. They pressed forward when everyone else retreated.

Black soldiers were not paid like white soldiers. Their food was rationed and they were kept almost unarmed since they were given almost no ammo (white soldiers feared blacks would turn on them).

Look at the difference in rate of pay. A Black soldier was paid $10 a month and $3 was deducted for clothes, leaving him $7, in contrast white soldiers were paid $13 a month and no deductions for clothes made.

Black soldiers were charged for nearly everything. When many of them ran out of ammo they were on their on, while white troops did not suffer.

Black soldiers were not allowed to gather with white soldiers, and every commander even for an all black regiment was white. Black troops were only allowed to serve after May 1, 1863, when the War Department created the Bureau of Colored Troops; because so many blacks sought entrance into the military).

When it came to prisoners of war and the treatment of black soldiers in particular, the black POWs seldom survived. Blacks were usually tortured for information, or shot on the spot.

The face of the enemy was not just seen at the end of the barrel of a rifle before a shot was fired, it was reflected in the actions of those who were in charge at wars conclusion. If blacks were allowed to be armed, their arms were now taken. They became slaves again, lied to and feared.

It was now 1865 and blacks have been freed from slavery. It was a time of celebration. Blacks could begin a life for themselves and families (if they could find them). The President is assassinated. What would that mean to be freed blacks? Would they once again have to return to slavery? Who would the blame fall on and what affect would it have for blacks.

Did African Americans find acceptance now that they were free? Life became even more difficult for them. Their greatest anguish would be the pain suffered internally. As black people sought to live lives of peace and happiness, they would find neither. Every disease and illness found in America was somehow the fault of black people.

In this country whose foundation was built on religious faith, exhibits very little for some of America's hardest working men and women to wear military uniforms. There were blacks who served in every war and fought for freedom, yet they were not seen as anything more than "coons, bucks, and niggas."

Men and women were only decorated and given honors long after they were dead (**meritoriously**).Some men and women choose death before dishonor. People of color were not allowed to march in parades celebrating their countries victories.

Here is food for thought. There was a black regiment that came to receive some acknowledgement because of its heroic deeds and somewhat showcased in the movie "Glory."

It was the 54th infantry, an all black regiment and their battle at Fort Wagner (1863), where over 300 black soldiers died in large part due to brutal hand to hand combat. It was their fighting that inspired other black regiments, bringing about the first Medal of Honor awarded to **William Carney.** As far as the world is concerned, he was nobody.

Whites believed that blacks would not make good soldiers. In October 1862, it was an African American infantry that would silence this belief. They were called the 1st Kansas Colored Volunteers keeping back attacking Confederate troops in the battle of Island Mound.

In 1863 the year of the Emancipation of blacks, there were over 14 Negro regiments in the fields who were ready for battle. At the battle of Port Hudson Louisiana, it was African Americans who bravely faced the enemy's gunfire in open ground. Although the attack failed, blacks proved that they were some of the best soldiers even under adverse conditions in May of 1863.

This same regiment would see battle again in July, just 2 months after their last confrontation at Honey springs Oklahoma, where they would again run into heavy battle under General James G. Blunt against confederate forces under General Douglas H. Cooper. We are told it was a bloody battle that went on for two hours before general Cooper would retreat. This black regiment was unrelenting and would not be moved, advancing to within yards of the confederate troops who turned and fled.

There was a battle that stands out above all others on April 12th, 1864, the battle of Fort Pillow, Tennessee. Many believed it was a battle that was a set-up to murder black soldiers. The confederates came against the Union held fortress with 2,500 men. The fortress had only 292 blacks and 285 white soldiers to defend it.

These men were given a chance to surrender. The fort was swarmed and they were driven down to the river into an ambush. There were only 62 men of the Colored Troop that survived. Since that day, there was a cry that would be heard from the Negro soldiers east of the Mississippi, "Remember Fort Pillows".

One third of all African Americans enlisted in the military loss their lives during the civil war. Of those executed for military and criminal offenses, it was found disproportionate numbers concerning black soldiers by 140%.

The great deeds done would not be enough to have black people seen in a better light. The world's problems would always fall on black shoulders. Black will always be the color of the enemy at home.

NOTES

Kings and Queens

Was it possible that there were people of color who were of noble decent? People, who ruled nations, governed people, people of prominence.
People who were certainly capable of loving, leading and establishing countries and ruling nations... Did such a people exist? Many of us know this to be so, but what happened to them, where are they today? They still exist but there are those who would like for us to believe otherwise.
Unfortunately one of the hardest things for black people to do is track their heritage back more than five or six generations. That does not mean it is impossible to do, however, there are a few things that we need to know as we trace. First it will not be an easy or pleasant task, and those who believe that black people are no more than lower class creatures will not accept these finding, because they are oppose to the thinking outside the box of racism.

We will look at several kings and queens who were people of color. They were not heathens, nor were they unlearned. Let us examine a few of these royal people and their treatment before and after their homeland was invaded by some Europeans.

We must ask ourselves the question, why do white Europeans think they have the exclusive right to dictate how people of other races should live, where they should live or even if they should live at all.

When it came to Africa, the thinking was that it was a savage land filled with animalistic beings that only ate raw meat, an unlearned, hostile and ignorant people devoid of common (white) sense.

How accurate was this thinking? It was not accurate at all, but it was not hard or uncommon to promote a perverse way of thinking and deem it right because it fits into a white agenda.

Were blacks the heathens and savages? We were lead to believe they were not capable of leading a home let alone a country? To the contrary, history shows they were rulers in many parts of the continent of Africa. They had political, spiritual and domestic lives.

Why would anyone teach an outright lie? This was no accident done through ignorance. It was willful and deliberate, as it was targeted intentionally to make black people think they have no history of greatness, and that at best they could only manage to be servants.

Lies are one reason whites did not want blacks to learn to read (this did not include all whites). They feared once blacks learned the truth about their captors, they would know "white" did not mean supreme. Blacks could read, write and communicate; it was the language of their land. When the colonies invaded Africa, it was not about teaching or sharing, but taking.

If you did not speak the language of the colony of the "New World" it was to their advantage. It became possible for them to put labels on everyone not like themselves. Were blacks the savages the European invaders said they were because they didn't walk, talk, live or act like white colonist?

I want you to know that there were more than just a few black men and women who were powerful leaders, as kings and queens in Africa. They were not heathens and savages that whites wanted the world of whites to believe, yet they even went as far as changing their ethnicity to fit white beliefs.

Sadly, these people of nobility were forced into slavery, but being kings and queens, and leaders of nations, some of them would not surrender to the brutality of any man and resisted bondage choosing death over oppression.

Listed here are a few black men and women of nobility, that white history would rather blacks not know about, since all heroes are white... Everyone knows that the villains are black. White represents light and goodness while black represents darkness and evil. **Darkness is a condition of the heart, not the color of the skin!**

Listed here are people of greatness, who are also people of color. You will also note that there were wars among African tribes and many died as a result of doing battle with other tribes. Those allowed to live were placed into servitude, particularly the men.

Kings

Tenkamenin, King of Ghana 1037-1075: Ghana reached its height of greatness during his reign in large part due to his management of the gold trade across the Sahara desert into West Africa. His kingdom flourished economically. It was said that his greatest strength was in government. He was a king that listened to his people, and no one was denied an audience with him and could remain with him until satisfied that justice was done (does not sound like a heathen to me). His tolerance made his reign one of the greatest models for African rule.

Mansa Kankan Mussa, King of Mali 1306-1332: during his reign, he was called colorful and flamboyant because he did everything on a grand scale. He was a scholar and businessman, and in 1324 he led his people on the hadj (a holy pilgrimage from Timbuktu to Mecca). His caravan consisted of 72,000 people, that he led safely across the Sahara desert and back a distance of more than 6,496 miles. It was because of this, that Mansa Mussa gained the respect of scholars and traders throughout Europe as one of the world's largest and wealthiest empires (it would not be long before they would return wanting to trade for more than goods).

Sunni Ali Ber King of Songhay 1464-1492: when he came into power, Songhay was a small kingdom in the western part of Sudan. During his 28 year reign, it grew into the largest and most powerful empire of West Africa (it was during this time that the slave trades were beginning to develop through Europeans) Sunni Ali Ber built a remarkable army. He was ferocious in battle and the warrior king won battle after battle. He defeated nomads, seized trade routes, took villages and expanded his domain. He captured Timbuktu and making Songhay a major center of commerce.

Ja Ja King of Opobo: ruled also during the same time as Sunni Ali Ber. Jubo Jubogha (JaJa's true name), was forced into slavery at the age of 12. He gained his freedom while still young and posed as a trader known as Ja Ja to the Europeans. He became the chief of his people and head of his Eastern Nigerian

City state of Bonny. As years passed, the European governments (British) attempted to gain control of Nigerian trade. Ja Ja resisted fiercely to all outside control, which lead to his exile at the age of 70 to the West Indies.

Idris Alooma Sultan of Bornu 1580-1617: was a devout Moslem (here is a black man who was not only literate but also had a religion) he replaced tribal laws with Moslem law. He as well, made a trip to Mecca early in his reign. He was a military as well as a religious man.

Shamba Bolongogo African King of peace 1600-1620: during his 20 year reign, he was called the greatest monarch of the Congo. He had no greater desire than to preserve peace, quoted as saying" kill neither man, woman, or child, are they not the children of Chembe (God), and have not the right to live?" His government was democratic and was divided into sectors which included military, judicial, and administrative branches and represented all Bushongo people.

Osei Tutu King of Asante 1680-1717: during his reign, the geographic size of Asante tripled.

Shaka, King of the Zulus 1818-1828: (*Son of Nandi**): he ruled for 10 years and was a strong military leader and innovator. He was noted for revolutionizing 19th century Bantu warfare by first grouping regiments by age, and training his men to use standard weapons and special tactics. Shaka also developed the assegai (a short stabbing spear), and marched his regiments in tight formation. Shaka's troops earned a reputation that many of his enemies would flee rather than fight them. He built a small Zulu tribe into a powerful nation of more than 1 million people, even uniting tribes to fight against colonial invaders.

Samory Toure the black Napoleon of the Sudan 1830-1900: the rise to power of Samory Toure began when his native Bissandugu was attacked and his mother was taken captive. After his appeal, Samory was allowed to take his mother's place. He later escaped and joined the army of King Bitike Souane of Torona and rose quickly through the ranks. Samory returned to Bissandugu where he was installed as King and defied the French expanding into Africa (one of the main purposes was taking Africans as slaves).

During the 18 year conflict with France, Samory continuously tormented the Europeans with his military abilities, strategy and tactics. His shrewd military prowess caused the greatest commanders of France to call him the black Napoleon of the Sudan.

Queens

What of the women of Africa the Nubian Queens, were there black women of nobility that we should know about? There are a number of black women who were leaders in Africa, here are just a few:

Amina, Queen of Zaria 1588-1589

Nzingha Amazon Queen of Matamba 1582-1663: she was of Angolan decent, and is known as a symbol of inspiration. She helped wage war against the savage slave hunting Europeans for more than 30 years. She was a member of a military group that formed a human shield against the Portuguese slave traders. She formed alliances with other foreign powers, pitting one against another to free Angolans from European domination. Sadly, her death in 1663 helped open the door for massive Portuguese slave trading.

Nandi Queen of Zululand 1778-1826: she was the mother of the great Zulu warrior Shaka. When she gave birth to this son, the kings other wives became jealous and bitter and pressured him to banish her and her child. Nandi would not let anything get in the way of her love for her child, and raised him as the royal heir. She later regained acceptance and her reward was a son who would be king.

There were women also like **Nefertari** the wife of Rameses II

Nehanda, (Mbuya) grandmother of Zimbabwe: when the English invaded Zimbabwe in 1896 taking (an act of aggression), land and cattle. Who needs permission? They were white. Nehanda and other leaders declared war. She demonstrated remarkable leadership skills at a young age. She remains even today what she was then, the single most important person in the history of Zimbabwe.

There was **Tiye the Nubian Queen of ancient Egypt 1415-1340 B.C**.: It was said that she was not only black but beautiful and considered one of the most influential Queens to ever rule Kemet (Egypt). A princess of Nubian birth, she married the King of Kemetan (Amenhoptep III). She held the title of "Great Royal Wife". It was she that ruled behind the scene when her husband died and her three children reigned. The most famous of which was a young king named Tutankhamen.

Yaa Asantewa of the Ashanti Empire: her history is known throughout Ghana. Her people feared to go into battle against the whites to rescue their king. She let the chiefs know that if they were afraid to go forth, then she and the other women would not hesitate to go into battle, saying they would fight until the last of them fall on the battlefield. Her speech had some affect and some men joined her in this battle for freedom.

For months, the Ashanti people lead by Yaa Asantewe, fought bravely and kept the whites in their fort until the British sent troops numbering more than 1,400 soldiers. Yaa Asantewe and other leaders were captured and sent into exile. This was the last major war in Africa that was lead by a woman.

Take this one for the record books. In many instances where the rulers of countries have been people of color, whites have changed them and made them to be white. It is what their history showed, and this is what black people were made to believe since they had no other resource than white literature and beliefs. Whites did not want blacks to believe that they could be more than sub-servants to the white race. For instance, one of the best known women in history was Cleopatra, but was she the woman white history has portrayed her as?

Cleopatra rose to the throne at the tender age of 17 from 69-30 BC: she was the seventh matriarch to bear this name. This young queen is always portrayed as a white woman. She was a woman of Greek and African descent and by white standards this made her black. All the heroes to whites had to be white and villains had to be black or dark, of course dark represents only evil, at least to the racist.

Cleopatra mastered many languages and African dialects and her fame would reach far beyond the borders of Egypt. As she strived to elevate Egypt to world supremacy, she enlisted the military services of two great Roman leaders named, Julius Caesar and later Mark Antony, convincing them to relinquish their Roman allegiances and fight on behalf of Egypt. Unfortunately, each of them met with death before she could see the dreams of her conquest realized. She would take her own life not long after, ending the life of one of Africa's most celebrated queens in the history of Egypt.

By white standards, I suppose these men and women of royalty had nothing to offer humanity. As people of color, we must recognized our place in history, and not accept past truths of what we are told. Instead, investigate for ourselves what is really true.

NOTES

See No Evil

All of us are familiar with the three little monkeys that sit side by side. One covered his eyes, another his ears and the third covered his mouth. What message are they relating to us, and what did it symbolize?

Could this be the true symbol for America and how Americans deal with life as a whole? Is this the unconscious belief of America? It has been said "don't ask don't tell". It is better to turn a deaf ear to many of the things that take place than to involve oneself, for fear of potential harm. It is better not to look than to see and have to get involved.

For hundreds of years if not thousands, this was a prevailing thought by those who were in the seat of power. Please take this thought to heart. Just certain people have power does not make them right.

It is always easier to choose what has been commonly called the lesser of two evils, but the point should be made that the choice still remains evil.

Americans, white in particular, have for hundreds of years done a grievous wrong against blacks, and yet took the approach that it could be justified and deemed right. That it was not evil to slay black people because, they in fact were not human at all and therefore not evil. To them, blacks have no souls.

A dog was treated better than a black person, whites loved their pets. **Even today, there is more being done to protect animal rights then focusing on human rights**.

As we talk about American history, we must seek the truth, the whole true and everything that is the truth. The truth of which I speak should include (not exclude) the history of blacks, but in telling the truth, it will not paint a very pretty picture of white people. Truth be told, there should be no need for black history or white history, it should just be history, but since the truth has been constantly hidden, diluted and very lopsided when told, it became necessary to unplug the bottle that held the truth, never to be sealed again.

The things we present here are not done with the intent to inflame, antagonize or to make blacks or whites angry, however, it might do just that. Even as I am writing about this, it angers me, but the anger I have is to be counted towards aggressively pursuing continual change.

It is my hope this book will help us all to see that the enemy has never been black people. But what would it take in order for them to get to that point?

Some have asked, why the need for change now? Everything was fine as it was. People were law abiding citizens, crimes were being punished and for the most part everybody was happy. Not everyone, however.

White America had buried its head in the sand, not wanting to face its own indignity, but in 1965 things again began to change. It would be a change that the entire world would have to pay attention to, a time of civil disobedience, an era that rang out loudly it is time for change.

A young civil rights leader was coming into prominence, a man who truly believed that all men were created equal in the sight of God. He was not the first man to fight for these rights and certainly not the last. This man was Dr. Martin Luther King, Jr.

Dr. King had a dream that all men could get along no matter what the color of their skin, religion, or place of origin.

Sadly, there were those who fought against the inalienable rights of black people to be treated not only as human beings, but equal to all other people under the law (the danger here was that the law was open to interpretation, white interpretation).

When it came to black people, the usual laws did not apply. That which was considered evil, vile or cruel, if done to a white person, was not seen that way at all when it came to black people.

History seems to always repeat itself. The Egyptians had a fear when the Jews who were their slaves began to out number them. Their solution being, kill them off and make it unbearable for them, so that they would not reproduce (***Exod.1: 8-22***). There is nothing new under the sun.

If things continue as they do today with no change, black people will have by the year 2019 continued to suffer at the hands of white people for 500+ years.

Would conditions ever change for these imported people who had been stripped of their identities, homes, dignity, culture and human rights to families? Would America ever wake up and confess to its wrong done to its African American populace?

Let us look again at the civil right movement of the 60's. Why did this have to take place? America was the home of the free, brave, and the place where the huddled masses could come and find fame, fortune and opportunity.

America was the place we were told that welcomed ethnicity and diversity. Were these things true or were they just surface dressing?

This statement was true, but only for those who volunteered to leave the land of their birth and start a new life in what was called America.

What about those who were not given that same choice, those who were snatched away from everything they knew and loved, what about them? Could they enjoy the same lifestyles as those who came over willingly?

By the time the civil rights act was signed in 1964 by President Lyndon Johnson, black people were suffering under the "**Jim Crow Laws**". The laws of segregation were enforced from 1876 through 1965, so by that time, black people had been enslaved for 346 years. A slave was someone who could not enjoy the same freedoms as every other human being.

Why did this bills' passage take place at that time? What was America's reason for change when its approach to life was so deeply rooted in the "see no evil" (slavery) principal?

Things are not nearly as appalling when we do not know or care to know about them. It was the "out of sight out of mind" theory. After all, blacks were now allowed to walk the streets with white people, eat at certain restaurants, and attended separate schools, but they were warned that they could not look up at or speak to whites unless told to do so (the penalty for doing so could be anything from a beating to a brutal death).

Were these the laws (ways) of a loving God or corrupt men? They were not of God. As history has demonstrated, it is not easy to be black growing up in America.

The fight for freedom continues today. We fight for economical freedom; we fight for the freedom to live where our finances say we can afford to live. We are still fighting for the freedom of equal education. We fight still for equal justice under the law.

Are blacks just being paranoid, are we just seeking sympathy or pity? To believe this is first insulting to the memory of every black person who has been castrated, lynched, and burned alive. This would be like telling the Jews that their Holocaust did not happen. There is history to confirm and pictures to prove both incidents.

Am I saying the blacks and Jews have something in common? They did for a moment. Whites have embraced and accepted the Jews, but there has been no such acceptance of black people or their plight.

When I speak of other races I do so only as points of reference showing the dissimilarity of these races.

It was easy to accept and embrace the Jews, after all, the things that happened to them was not done by white America, but by Germans, Nazis who sought to purge the human race of everyone not like themselves (blond hair and blue eyes).

The Jewish nation fought to have the world recognize and not forget what happened to them. In like manner, black people seek to have America acknowledge what was done to them, and America must see the evil that was done.

It must also be said that the Jews were likewise owners and sellers of slaves as well. Let us be factual about it. They fit into the white European culture. How could a people who were so acquainted with suffering, grief and oppression cause it for blacks as well? History shows it was all about the money?

Americans have never wanted to see themselves as oppressors, wanting instead to see themselves as liberators. In the mind of most Americans, they have done no wrong, so therefore no apology is forthcoming to black people.

Why should America apologize to black people when they have not done so to the Nations they have invaded for democracy sake around the world?

The mistreatment done to black people was never about "justice" but "just us", complete domination and assimilation by Europeans.

When we hear the statement "see no evil" we can very well say it also means "see no wrong". America saw nothing wrong in the things they did to black people, and besides, it was done to help America's future economic growth. As **"they"** say, "the end justifies the means".

Thank God that even some white Americans, like the abolitionist before them, wearied of the abuse they saw. This became abundantly clear when the violence was televised and stared into the faces of so called God fearing people.

The violence could no longer be hidden on the back pages of America's conscience. Its horror has now taken center stage, being brought into living rooms around the world.

The date was March 7th, 1965, when a group of black marchers were attacked unprovoked, as they peacefully crossed the Edmund Pettus Bridge in Selma Alabama travelling to the state capital of Montgomery. What was done to them horrified as well as galvanized the nation. Finally, the sins of the parents would not become the sins of the children.

Now parents have to explain to a new generation why dogs were being put on women and children, why they are being clubbed in the streets, and water hoses sprayed in there faces. What had they done? Were they suffering because of crimes they had committed? Certainly it was more than just the skin they were in?

What was the cause of the entire stir? Was it because of some woman's refusal to give up a seat on a bus 10 years earlier?

Some would say yes. This movement was not about a seat on a bus, but about unequal treatment of blacks as a race of people. Rosa Parks was one of millions who wearied of the treatment of blacks.

Although that movement was non-violent and about civil disobedience, everyone participating was treated as if they were hardened criminals.

Who was it that set the stage for this violence in 1965? Law enforcement officers, even State Troopers helped ignite it. If law enforcement attacked black people with such viciousness, it was okay for the average citizen to join in, and at the very least they did nothing to discourage them.

Some whites were enraged not because of what took place in the lives of these black people, but a great rallying call came because three of their own, Michael Schwerner, Andrew Goodman, and James Chaney were murdered defending black peoples civil rights and their right to vote.

Economical empowerment, black people literally shut down the city in 1955. Although they were not treated as equals they were one of the country's largest consumers. Their money was one of the countries greatest stimuli's. They gave up riding mass transportation, and in doing so affected the cities finances, and this was totally unacceptable and would not be tolerated.

The lawmakers could not accept this boycotting, even trying to force them to comply and making their actions illegal. Blacks were being arrested for not spending their own money.

America had refused to look at black people seriously. We were not treated fairly, or justly, but white America had not paid attention to something they were doing. Black people learned a valuable lesson that money was their power.

Black people were being paid for some of the services they performed. Their pay was not close to the pay of whites, yet up until this time black people had not recognized or fully understood its power. Whites served the almighty dollar, as it had become their god, gaining strength beginning in 1619, when they first began to import blacks to this country.

If America was going to be brought down, it would come because of man's greed, and desire for money. Osama Bin Laden knew white America's thinking. This is why we are told he attacked the World Trade Center, which represented American Capitalism.

Nations around the world are now aware that they could break the back of America by hitting them in the thing they love most, and finances (money). The dollar is losing its value all around the world and America their credibility.

A predominately European Nation, such as America, refuses to see the evil it has done to its own people. Lives are a distant second to money in the U.S.

Slavery was believed necessary by all financial profiteers in its heyday. Though abolished today from the books, it is still very much alive, even thriving in America. If it were not so, we would have no need for agencies as EEOC (Equal Employment Opportunity Commission).

How does America get what it wants? It turns to the thing it knows best which happens to be, violence, terror and propaganda.

NOTES

Till Death

One of the most horrific crimes to take place did so in one of the most racially charged cities of the South. It was known for hatred towards blacks. Mississippi was a city that believed in the laws of Jim Crow which was used as its bible of racism. This town would soon rally around its own, a city that would embrace murderers and resist truth.

It was the summer of 1955 when a young man Emmett Louis Till was sent from his home in Chicago to visit his cousins in the small town of Money, Mississippi. Emmett would find that life in the South was not like that of his home in the North. His time of joy would become his family's time of sorrow.

Racial tensions were high because of the court decision a year earlier concerning Brown verses the Board of Education passing in 1954 a law calling for desegregation. It was August 21st, when Emmett arrived in Money. On August 24th he and a couple of other teens went to a store (Bryant's grocery and meat market) to get some snacks.

It was there that Emmett showed his friends a photo of a female friend from back home that happened to be white. Emmett being young and only 14 was naive to the ways of the south. He was warned by his mother to mind his manners when it came to white people, but as with so many young people, the words did not resonance with him. He simply saw life as unprejudiced from North to South. There were restrictions in the North, but people were more tolerant of its black people.

  Emmett was not aware that a little thing such as a dare would lead to his death. In the south where blacks did not speak to whites unless they were spoken to, Emmett was dared to speak to the white woman who was in the store. She also happened to be the wife of the store owner. Her name was Carolyn, her husband was Roy. Emmett's friends dared him to speak to the woman in the store. He was known to be someone who liked to joke and have fun, so he took the dare. What resulted would be known around the world.

  After Emmett made his purchase it was alleged that he said, "Bye baby" as he was leaving. Another version says that he whistled at her (it was said that Emmett had a lisp and this could have contributed to what was thought to be a whistle).

Whistling at a white woman in the south was according to whites, a lynching offense. Word spread around town as to what was believed said. When Carolyn's husband returned to town, he was told what had allegedly taken place and was not having it. Something had to be done, what would people think with his wife's honor at stake.

The major fuel for the fire of justification came from the Carolyn Bryant herself. She said Emmett grabbed her by the waist and asked her for a date, even adding unmentionable words according to her.

Roy and his brother J.W. Milam decided to teach this black boy a lesson. On August 27th at about 12:30 am, they kidnapped him from his uncle's house taking him from his bed, to a neighboring plantation in Sunflower County where witnesses said he was brutally beat and shot. His body was thrown into the Tallahatchie River.

After his body was discovered, the truth of what was done to him was partially revealed. Not until the year 2004, the real truth was found when his body was exhumed and an autopsy was performed detailing the horror of his death.

This young man was beaten (pistol-whipped) beyond recognition as was seen when he was given an open casket funeral. He was shot, had his eye gouged out and a 75 pound cotton gin fan was hang around his neck when his body was cast into the river. (Look at the message, and invention made by a black man, that helped white people to continue oppression of black people now hangs about the neck of a murdered black child by white men).

Later it was revealed by the killers that part of the beating was due to the picture they had found in Emmett's pocket of a white girl. Remember these were adults beating a child to death.

Emmett's body could only be identified by the ring on his finger which belonged to his dad who was hanged in the Army for the rape of two women and the killing of a third. (This fact the Till family had no knowledge of until it was presented at the trial of the men who murdered Emmett).

These evil men had also threatened Emmett's uncle telling him not to speak a word about them taking his nephew out of his home. The uncle suggested they just beat him right there but not take him away fearing for his nephews safety.

The country again would be divided along racial lines. After the killers of Emmett were arrested, many blacks believed that the law just might be fair. Some whites even cried out that the people who did this should pay, but it would not be so.

No good white person would side against one of their own for some dead black. They had to protect their own at any cost. This crime was not one that was an isolated incident, but came to life because one mother refused to let herself be threatened. To Mamie Till it was principle.

Emmett was buried on September 6th on same day Roy and J.W were indicted by a grand jury. The trial of Roy and J.W. began on September 19th. In an attempt to sway the public support that was gaining for the Till family, James Eastland a senator brought into the trial the events of Louis Tills death hoping to show that criminal behavior ran in the Till family. Nothing Emmett did was a crime, except in white eyes.

On September 23 an all white jury of 12 men acquitted both men in less than 67 minutes (they had come to a decision long before, taking a soda break to kill some time). The acquittal inflamed people all around the world, so much so that it was what pushed the civil rights movement into the forefront of the nation. It became the new rallying call for justice.

Were these men guilty? Without a doubt; even selling their story of what they did to Look Magazine. Knowing they could not be tried again for the same crime because of a clause in the law called double jeopardy.

Racism lives on in Mississippi. In 2006, a historical marker placed at the sight where Emmett died was defaced, and stolen in August 2007. Another was put in its place, but what a sad commentary for that city. They want to forget what was done, but we must not let Emmett's death or the countless other deaths be in vain.

The crimes of Mississippi happen in every state. There is an Emmett Till story that could be told by families everywhere. A law taken off the book does not mean that it has been removed from people's hearts.

NOTES

They Can't Handle the Truth

I have heard a saying some time ago that emphasized a certain path of thinking when it was said, "know the truth and the truth will make you free." Is this freedom being spoken of a freedom from something or a freedom to something?

Is this truth on a moral, economical, or spiritual basis? What and who does it apply to? Truth, it would seem is in the mind of the one who is delivering it. For instance, a lie can become the truth to the one who tells it. They draw on their own perception of what they want to believe is true.

Much of what we call mental illness stems from this type of thinking. Now here is the catch. All of us suffer from mental illness to some degree; some more than others, but all none the less. It is our way to go about doing whatever we think is right (what we feel best suits us personally).

We argue over what is right and wrong and who has the right to decide what it is. We have devised saying like, "the needs of the many out weigh the needs of the few"; in order to help justify skewed thinking.

Every religious organization has as its foundation what they call truth. Can they all be wrong, or can they all be right? This is the question that still baffles people, causing arguments, wars, hatred and death.

Man's greatest failure is his inability to accept differences. He is driven to be a god, and he desires to be the superior (Supreme) being. What he cannot have he destroys. He goes to war to have more, to get more and control more.

The preservation of life means little to those who are lead by the need for greed. This is a truth that many would like not to hear or know about.

Hard hearts (arrogance, hate, pride, racism), have lead to and continues to lead man down the road to self loathing. Slavery, the forceful imprisonment of innocent people for profit, has been one of man's greatest ills. Anyone who believed that owning another human being was justifiable and righteous, cannot know the truth.

Everyone likes to talk about what they call the truth, but what is truth? Is it the absence of a lie? Then how would we define a lie? Is it the opposite of the truth?

People are liars by nature. You do not have to teach anyone how to lie, they do so almost instinctively. People lie in order to accomplish set goals. People lie because it is easy and convenient. It seems to take less time to lie than to tell the truth (or be honest, to have moral value.) A liar can tell the truth as well as a person who tells the truth can lie. So what is the difference? Are they one in the same?

Man began his life on the road of truth but quickly exchanged it for a path of lies (of his own choosing). Some lies are done through ignorance, while some lies are taught as truth by people who knowingly pervert known facts to attain hidden agendas. This is not uncommon for those who are power hungry. The opportunity of slavery was a gold mine for the opportunist.

When it came to black people, lies upon lies have been told, fabricated, and promoted concerning them, and if you tell a lie long enough it begins to sound like the truth. There are those of course that sprinkle just enough truth in their lie to come off believable to the listeners. When people cannot handle the truth, they make up their own version (lie).

For instance, it was said to be fact that black people had tails; that they had a special bone in their leg that made them run faster than white people. It was also said that blacks out numbered whites in jail, and that they are more violent than whites. If anyone is interested and did the research, they would find that none of these things were true. Sadly, many of our European brothers and sisters, who do not read or research for themselves, have accepted and believed the lie they were told often without question.

Whites as well as blacks are not comfortable with having the truth revealed to them. To do so, means history would have to be rewritten. To put it another way, we were lied to. This is a wake up call to the generations coming. Do not believe anything that you do not research for yourself, truth does not come without conflict.

This country (the New World, The Americas, and the USA) is still wandering around in moral darkness. We know how we should treat one another but refuse to do so. We are in spiritual chaos because of spiritual disconnecting from God. Man's greed leads him to hurt, harm and kill in order to feed his need for more.

What is the truth that we should know? There are those who say the freedom that blacks should seek is spiritual. They were meant to be slaves forever, and should take comfort in knowing they have served the human race in the capacity for which they were created. If this is true, then why lie to people saying all men are created equal?

The greatest strength of the white people has been their ability to lie. Not because they had to. They wanted to mask the truth and hide it from not only its African American people but all people. It is the power of the few to dictate the choices of the many. It is the belief that they (the world at large) cannot handle the truth.

How would the masses respond if they knew that black people had done nothing to incur the resentment, the bullying, the hate and murder put upon them by white people?

How would they respond once they knew that blacks have been hunted down and brutally slaughtered for reasons that were no more than demonic and evil? Could they handle that truth, or continue to pervert it and justify it? From everything promoted today, such as the televising of black crimes, to the statistics given, the American people are still flooded with pictures that suggest the greatest crimes being committed are done so to black people.

    White America is not ready to accept the truth about itself. Anyone who disagrees with their thinking is found to be an enemy of America, someone who should be watched carefully as they may be a threat to national security.

    Fear is the new truth. America will hide the facts and *propaganda* fear. People are best controlled by fear and punishment. Whites controlled black people using these as their tools. Light will ultimately shine in the darkness revealing the evil in the hearts of man. Evil will not go unpunished, there is cause an effect and, everything is connected.

    There is a movie I watched some time ago that I found particularly interesting. It was a "what if" kind of a movie. It did not see much money at the box office. As a matter of fact, it was considered a flop. It told a remarkable story, a controversial story depending on one's view.

The movie was called "White Man's Burden". I am sure it did not enjoy success because of its theme and subject matter. I do not want to give everything away, in hopes that you will see and evaluate the movie for yourself.

The movie tells the story about what it would be like if all the whites were to be put in the position that blacks held for over a hundred years, and blacks were the ones running the country.

Almost immediately, I know people were offended, they became angered at the very thought of blacks having what they considered "white power." Certainly it is not an easy movie to watch, but I recommend that everyone see it. This movie was played down as far as its subject matter and it seems to me that it was raced in and out of the market for fear of what it talked about. Every negative thing that could be thought of concerning what whites want to believe about blacks would flood their mind. Whites do not believe blacks could, would, or should be leaders of anything.

Hollywood wants to see what they want to see. This was not their kind of movie, and was not bankable. Many who did see it were displeased, sighting the impossibility of such a thing ever taking place.

Whites have placed in the consciousness of men that any way other than the white way is wrong and should not be tolerated. The reason for this is simple. Our European Americans cannot handle the truth, other than the one they have created for themselves.

It is easy for them to believe that America was somehow built by the labor of their hands when in fact it was not built by them at all. Native Americans, Chinese, and black Americans were harvested and forced to do the bidding of white oppressors, who through torture, rape, murder and lies have built a nation of racist, warmongers and murderers. It is most difficult for them to face the monster they have created through greed and selfishness.

NOTES

Please read over the following documents carefully, to judge for yourself as to whether or not the mindset of the writers along with their intentions was about liberating or oppressing? How did each of these great writings written by leaders affect all men?

Three of the best known documents that helped shape America are on the following pages (i-xxiii), The Declaration of Independence (the breaking away from British servitude), The Emancipation Proclamation and lastly, I included the Fugitive Slave Act.

The contents of each, represents the beliefs of those who penned them and those who accepted and passed them into law.

Did these acts show or embody a true view of all people, meaning the rich and the poor, male and female, black and white?

The question becomes, who stood to gain the most from the enactment of each of them? It certainly was not black Americans.

Black people were taken advantage of. Was this because they are weak? Not so, as many whites believed, they are meek. Fear becomes the breeding ground for hate, and the Fugitive Slave Act came into existence because of economic fear.

    Please read each of them carefully and evaluate them according to human rational reasoning. Are these the doings of God fearing men who believed in a God of love? Does God love everyone but black people?

The Emancipation Proclamation

January 1, 1863

By the President of the United States of America:

A Proclamation.

Whereas, on the twenty-second day of September, in the year of our Lord one thousand eight hundred and sixty-two, a proclamation was issued by the President of the United States, containing, among other things, the following, to wit:

> "That on the first day of January, in the year of our Lord one thousand eight hundred and sixty-three, all persons held as slaves within any State or designated part of a State, the people whereof shall then be in rebellion against the United States, shall be then, thenceforward, and forever free; and the Executive Government of the United States, including the military and naval authority thereof, will recognize and maintain the freedom of such

persons, and will do no act or acts to repress such persons, or any of them, in any efforts they may make for their actual freedom.

"That the Executive will, on the first day of January aforesaid, by proclamation, designate the States and parts of States, if any, in which the people thereof, respectively, shall then be in rebellion against the United States; and the fact that any State, or the people thereof, shall on that day be, in good faith, represented in the Congress of the United States by members chosen thereto at elections wherein a majority of the qualified voters of such State shall have participated, shall, in the absence of strong countervailing testimony, be deemed conclusive evidence that such State, and the people thereof, are not then in rebellion against the United States."
Now, therefore I, Abraham Lincoln, President of the United States, by virtue of the power in me vested as Commander-in-Chief, of the Army and Navy of the

United States in time of actual armed rebellion against the authority and government of the United States, and as a fit and necessary war measure for suppressing said rebellion, do, on this first day of January, in the year of our Lord one thousand eight hundred and sixty-three, and in accordance with my purpose so to do publicly proclaimed for the full period of one hundred days, from the day first above mentioned, order and designate as the States and parts of States wherein the people thereof respectively, are this day in rebellion against the United States, the following, to wit:

Arkansas, Texas, Louisiana, (except the Parishes of St. Bernard, Plaquemines, Jefferson, St. John, St. Charles, St. James Ascension, Assumption, Terrebonne, Lafourche, St. Mary, St. Martin, and Orleans, including the City of New Orleans) Mississippi, Alabama, Florida, Georgia, South Carolina, North Carolina, and Virginia, (except the forty-eight counties designated as West Virginia, and also the counties of Berkley, Accomac, Northampton, Elizabeth City, York, Princess Ann, and Norfolk, including the cities of Norfolk and Portsmouth[)], and which excepted parts, are for the present, left precisely as if this proclamation were not issued.

And by virtue of the power, and for the purpose aforesaid, I do order and declare that all persons held as slaves within said designated States, and parts of States, are, and henceforward shall be free; and that the Executive government of the United States, including the military and naval authorities thereof, will recognize and maintain the freedom of said persons.

And I hereby enjoin upon the people so declared to be free to abstain from all violence, unless in necessary self-defense; and I recommend to them that, in all cases when allowed, they labor faithfully for reasonable wages.

And I further declare and make known, that such persons of suitable condition, will be received into the armed service of the United States to garrison forts, positions, stations, and other places, and to man vessels of all sorts in said service.

And upon this act, sincerely believed to be an act of justice, warranted by the Constitution, upon military necessity, I invoke the considerate judgment of mankind, and the gracious favor of Almighty God.

In witness whereof, I have hereunto set my hand and caused the seal of the United States to be affixed.

Done at the City of Washington, this first day of
January, in the year of our Lord one thousand eight
Hundred and sixty three, and of the Independence of the
United States of America the eighty-seventh.

By the President: ABRAHAM LINCOLN
WILLIAM H. SEWARD, Secretary of State.

The Declaration of Independence

July 4th 1776

We hold these truths to be self-evident, that all men are created equal, that they are endowed by their Creator with certain unalienable rights, that among these are life, liberty and the pursuit of happiness.

That to secure these rights, governments are instituted among men, deriving their just powers from the consent of the governed.

That whenever any form of government becomes destructive to these ends, it is the right of the people to alter or to abolish it, and to institute new government, laying its foundation on such principles and organizing its powers in such form, as to them shall seem most likely to effect their safety and happiness.

Prudence, indeed, will dictate that governments long established should not be changed for light and transient causes; and accordingly all experience hath shown that mankind are more disposed to suffer, while evils are sufferable, than to right themselves by abolishing the forms to which they are accustomed.

But when a long train of abuses and usurpations, pursuing invariably the same object evinces a design to reduce them under absolute despotism, it is their right, it is their duty, to throw off such government, and to provide new guards for their future security. --Such has been the patient sufferance of these colonies; and such is now the necessity which constrains them to alter their former systems of government.

The history of the present King of Great Britain is a history of repeated injuries and usurpations, all having in direct object the establishment of an absolute tyranny over these states.

To prove this, let facts be submitted to a candid world.

He has refused his assent to laws, the most wholesome and necessary for the public good.

He has forbidden his governors to pass laws of immediate and pressing importance, unless suspended in their operation till his assent should be obtained; and when so suspended, he has utterly neglected to attend to them.

He has refused to pass other laws for the accommodation of large districts of people, unless those people would relinquish the right of representation in the legislature, a right inestimable to them and formidable to tyrants only.

He has called together legislative bodies at places unusual, uncomfortable, and distant from the depository of their public records, for the sole purpose of fatiguing them into compliance with his measures.

He has dissolved representative houses repeatedly, for opposing with manly firmness his invasions on the rights of the people.

He has refused for a long time, after such dissolutions, to cause others to be elected; whereby the legislative powers, incapable of annihilation, have returned to the people at large for their exercise; the state remaining in the meantime exposed to all the dangers of invasion from without, and convulsions within.

He has endeavored to prevent the population of these states; for that purpose obstructing the laws for naturalization of foreigners; refusing to pass others to encourage their migration hither, and raising the conditions of new appropriations of lands.

He has obstructed the administration of justice, by refusing his assent to laws for establishing judiciary powers.

He has made judges dependent on his will alone, for the tenure of their offices, and the amount and payment of their salaries.

He has erected a multitude of new offices, and sent hither swarms of officers to harass our people, and eat out their substance.

He has kept among us, in times of peace, standing armies without the consent of our legislature.

He has affected to render the military independent of and superior to civil power.

He has combined with others to subject us to a jurisdiction foreign to our constitution, and unacknowledged by our laws; giving his assent to their acts of pretended legislation:

For quartering large bodies of armed troops among us:

For protecting them, by mock trial, from punishment for any murders which they should commit on the inhabitants of these states:

For cutting off our trade with all parts of the world:

For imposing taxes on us without our consent:

For depriving us in many cases, of the benefits of trial by jury:

For transporting us beyond seas to be tried for pretended offenses:

For abolishing the free system of English laws in a neighboring province, establishing therein an arbitrary government, and enlarging its boundaries so as to render it at once an example and fit instrument for introducing the same absolute rule in these colonies:

For taking away our charters, abolishing our most valuable laws, and altering fundamentally the forms of our governments:

For suspending our own legislatures, and declaring themselves invested with power to legislate for us in all cases whatsoever.

He has abdicated government here, by declaring us out of his protection and waging war against us.

He has plundered our seas, ravaged our coasts, burned our towns, and destroyed the lives of our people.

He is at this time transporting large armies of foreign mercenaries to complete the works of death, desolation and tyranny, already begun with circumstances of cruelty and perfidy scarcely paralleled in the most barbarous ages, and totally unworthy the head of a civilized nation.

He has constrained our fellow citizens taken captive on the high seas to bear arms against their country, to become the executioners of their friends and brethren, or to fall themselves by their hands.

He has excited domestic insurrections amongst us, and has endeavored to bring on the inhabitants of our frontiers, the merciless Indian savages, whose known rule of warfare, is undistinguished destruction of all ages, sexes and conditions.

In every stage of these oppressions we have petitioned for redress in the most humble terms: our repeated petitions have been answered only by repeated injury. A prince, whose character is thus marked by every act which may define a tyrant, is unfit to be the ruler of a free people.

Nor have we been wanting in attention to our British brethren. We have warned them from time to time of attempts by their legislature to extend an unwarrantable jurisdiction over us. We have reminded them of the circumstances of our emigration and settlement here. We have appealed to their native justice and magnanimity, and we have conjured them by the ties of our common kindred to disavow these usurpations, which, would inevitably interrupt our connections and correspondence. We must, therefore, acquiesce in the necessity, which denounces our separation, and hold them, as we hold the rest of mankind, enemies in war, in peace friends.

We, therefore, the representatives of the United States of America, in General Congress, assembled, appealing to the Supreme Judge of the world for the rectitude of our intentions, do, in the name, and by the authority of the good people of these colonies, solemnly publish and declare, that these united colonies are, and of right ought to be free and independent states; that they are absolved from all allegiance to the British Crown, and that all political connection between them and the state of Great Britain, is and ought to be totally dissolved; and that as free and independent states, they have full power to levy war, conclude peace, contract alliances, establish commerce, and to do all other acts and things which independent states may of right do. And for the support of this declaration, with a firm reliance on the protection of Divine Providence, we mutually pledge to each other our lives, our fortunes and our sacred honor.

New Hampshire: Josiah Bartlett, William Whipple, Matthew Thornton

Massachusetts: John Hancock, Samual Adams, John Adams, Robert Treat Paine, Elbridge Gerry

Rhode Island: Stephen Hopkins, William Ellery

Connecticut: Roger Sherman, Samuel Huntington, William Williams, Oliver Wolcott

New York: William Floyd, Philip Livingston, Francis Lewis, Lewis Morris

New Jersey: Richard Stockton, John Witherspoon, Francis Hopkinson, John Hart, Abraham Clark

Pennsylvania: Robert Morris, Benjamin Rush, Benjamin Franklin, John Morton, George Clymer, James Smith, George Taylor, James Wilson, George Ross

Delaware: Caesar Rodney, George Read, Thomas McKean

Maryland: Samuel Chase, William Paca, Thomas Stone, Charles Carroll of Carrollton

Virginia: George Wythe, Richard Henry Lee, Thomas Jefferson, Benjamin Harrison, Thomas Nelson, Jr., Francis Lightfoot Lee, Carter Braxton

North Carolina: William Hooper, Joseph Hewes, John Penn

South Carolina: Edward Rutledge, Thomas Heyward, Jr., Thomas Lynch, Jr., Arthur Middleton

Georgia: Button Gwinnett, Lyman Hall, George Walton.

"What To The Slave Is The 4th Of July?" FREDERICK DOUGLASS SPEECH, 1852

Fellow citizens, pardon me, allow me to ask, why am I called upon to speak here today? What have I, or those I represent, to do with your national independence? Are the great principles of political freedom and of natural justice, embodied in that Declaration of Independence, extended to us? and am I, therefore, called upon to bring our humble offering to the national altar, and to confess the benefits and express devout gratitude for the blessings resulting from your independence to us?

Would to God, both for your sakes and ours, that an affirmative answer could be truthfully returned to these questions! Then would my task be light, and my burden easy and delightful. For who is there so cold that a nation's sympathy could not warm him? Who so obdurate and dead to the claims of gratitude that would not thankfully acknowledge such priceless benefits? Who so stolid and selfish that would not give his voice to swell the hallelujahs of a nation's jubilee, when the chains of servitude had been torn from his limbs? I am not that man. In a case like that the dumb might eloquently speak and the "lame man leap as a hart

But such is not the state of the case. I say it with a sad sense of the disparity between us. am not included within the pale of this glorious anniversary! Your high independence only reveals the immeasurable distance between us. The blessings in which you, this day, rejoice are not enjoyed in common. The rich inheritance of justice, liberty, prosperity, and independence bequeathed by your fathers is shared by you, not by me. The sunlight that brought light and healing to you has brought stripes and death to me. This Fourth of July is yours, not mine. You may rejoice, I must mourn. To drag a man in fetters into the grand illuminated temple of liberty, and call upon him to join you in joyous anthems, were inhuman mockery and sacrilegious irony. Do you mean, citizens, to mock me by asking me to speak today? If so, there is a parallel to your conduct. And let me warn that it is dangerous to copy the example of nation whose crimes, towering up to heaven, were thrown down by the breath of the Almighty, burying that nation in irrevocable ruin! I can today take up the plaintive lament of a peeled and woe-smitten people.

"By the rivers of Babylon, there we sat down. Yea! We wept when we remembered Zion. We hanged our harps upon the willows in the midst thereof. For there, they that carried us away captive, required of us a song; and they who wasted us required of us mirth, saying, Sing us one of the songs of Zion. How can we sing the Lord's song in a strange land? If I forget thee, O Jerusalem, let my right hand forget her cunning. If do not remember thee, let my tongue cleave to the roof of my mouth."

Fellow citizens, above your national, tumultuous joy, I hear the mournful wail of millions! Whose chains, heavy and grievous yesterday, are, today, rendered more intolerable by the jubilee shouts that reach them. If I do forget, if I do not faithfully remember those bleeding children of sorry this day, "may my right hand cleave to the roof of my mouth"! To forget them, to pass lightly over their wrongs, and to chime in with the popular theme would be treason most scandalous and shocking, and would make me a reproach before God and the world.

My subject, then, fellow citizens, is American slavery. I shall see this day and its popular characteristics from the slave's point of view. Standing there identified with the American bondman, making his wrongs mine. I do not hesitate to declare with all my soul that the character and conduct of this nation never looked blacker to me than on this Fourth of July! Whether we turn to the declarations of the past or to the professions of the present, the conduct of the nation seems equally hideous and revolting. America is false to the past, false to the present, and solemnly binds herself to be false to the future. Standing with God and the crushed and bleeding slave on this occasion, I will, in the name of humanity which is outraged, in the name of liberty which is fettered, in the name of the Constitution and the Bible which are disregarded and trampled upon, dare to call in question and to denounce, with all the emphasis I can command, everything that serves to perpetuate slavery-the great sin and shame of America! "I will not equivocate, I will not excuse"; I will use the severest language I can command; and yet not one word shall escape me that any man, whose judgment is not blinded by prejudice, shall not confess to be right and just....

For the present, it is enough to affirm the equal manhood of the Negro race. Is it not as astonishing that, while we are plowing, planting, and reaping, using all kinds of mechanical tools, erecting houses, constructing bridges, building ships, working in metals of brass, iron, copper, and secretaries, having among us lawyers doctors, ministers, poets, authors, editors, orators, and teachers; and that, while we are engaged in all manner of enterprises common to other men, digging gold in California, capturing the whale in the Pacific, feeding sheep and cattle on the hillside, living, moving, acting, thinking, planning, living in families as husbands, wives, and children, and above all, confessing and worshiping the Christian's God, and looking hopefully for life and immortality beyond the grave, we are called upon to prove that we are men!...

The Fugitive Slave Act,

September 18, 1850

Section 1: Be it enacted by the Senate and House of Representatives of the United States of America in Congress assembled, That the persons who have been, or may hereafter be, appointed commissioners, in virtue of any act of Congress, by the Circuit Courts of the United States, and Who, in consequence of such appointment, are authorized to exercise the powers that any justice of the peace, or other magistrate of any of the United States, may exercise in respect to offenders for any crime or offense against the United States, by arresting, imprisoning, or bailing the same under and by the virtue of the thirty-third section of the act of the twenty-fourth of September seventeen hundred and eighty-nine, entitled "An Act to establish the judicial courts of the United States" shall be, and are hereby, authorized and required to exercise and discharge all the powers and duties conferred by this act.

Section 2: And be it further enacted, That the Superior Court of each organized Territory of the United States shall have the same power to appoint commissioners to take acknowledgments of bail and affidavits, and to take depositions of witnesses in civil causes, which is now possessed by the Circuit Court of the United States; and all commissioners who shall hereafter be appointed for such purposes by the Superior Court of any organized Territory of the United States, shall possess all the powers, and exercise all the duties, conferred by law upon the commissioners appointed by the Circuit Courts of the United States for similar purposes, and shall moreover exercise and discharge all the powers and duties conferred by this act.

Section 3: And be it further enacted, That the Circuit Courts of the United States shall from time to time enlarge the number of the commissioners, with a view to afford reasonable facilities to reclaim fugitives from labor, and to the prompt discharge of the duties imposed by this act.

Section 4: And be it further enacted, That the commissioners above named shall have concurrent jurisdiction with the judges of the Circuit and District Courts of the United States, in their respective circuits and districts within the several States, and the judges of the Superior Courts of the Territories, severally and collectively, in term-time and vacation; shall grant certificates to such claimants, upon satisfactory proof being made, with authority to take and remove such fugitives from service or labor, under the restrictions herein contained, to the State or Territory from which such persons may have escaped or fled.

Section 5: And be it further enacted, That it shall be the duty of all marshals and deputy marshals to obey and execute all warrants and precepts issued under the provisions of this act, when to them directed; and should any marshal or deputy marshal refuse to receive such warrant, or other process, when tendered, or to use all proper means diligently to execute the same, he shall, on conviction thereof, be fined in the sum of one thousand dollars, to the use of such claimant, on the motion of such claimant, by the Circuit or District Court for the district of such marshal; and after arrest of such fugitive, by such marshal or his deputy, or whilst at any time in his custody under the provisions of this act, should such fugitive escape, whether with or without the assent of such marshal or his deputy, such marshal shall be liable, on his official bond, to be prosecuted for the benefit of such claimant, for the full value of the service or labor of said fugitive in the State, Territory, or District whence he escaped: and the better to enable the said commissioners, when thus appointed, to execute their duties faithfully and efficiently, in conformity with the requirements of the Constitution of the United States and of this act, they are hereby authorized and empowered, within their counties respectively, to appoint, in writing under their hands, any one or more suitable persons, from time to time, to execute all such warrants and other process as may be issued by them in the lawful performance of their respective duties; with authority to such commissioners, or the persons to be appointed by them, to execute process as aforesaid, to summon and call to their aid the bystanders, or posse comitatus of the proper county, when necessary to ensure a faithful observance of the clause of the Constitution referred to, in conformity with the provisions of this act; and all good citizens are hereby commanded to aid and assist in the prompt and efficient execution of this law, whenever their services may be required, as aforesaid, for that purpose; and said warrants shall run, and be executed by said officers, any where in the State within which they are issued.

Section 6: And be it further enacted, That when a person held to service or labor in any State or Territory of the United States, has heretofore or shall hereafter escape into another State or Territory of the United States, the person or persons to whom such service or labor may be due, or his, her, or their agent or attorney, duly authorized, by power of attorney, in writing, acknowledged and certified under the seal of some legal officer or court of the State or Territory in which the same may be executed, may pursue and reclaim such fugitive person, either by procuring a warrant from some one of the courts, judges, or commissioners aforesaid, of the proper circuit, district, or county, for the apprehension of such fugitive from service or labor, or by seizing and arresting such fugitive, where the same can be done without process, and by taking, or causing such person to be taken, forthwith before such court, judge, or commissioner, whose duty it shall be to hear and determine the case of such claimant in a summary manner; and upon satisfactory proof being made, by deposition or affidavit, in writing, to be taken and certified by such court, judge, or commissioner, or by other satisfactory testimony, duly taken and certified by some court, magistrate, justice of the peace, or other legal officer authorized to administer an oath and take depositions under the laws of the State or Territory from which such person owing service or labor may have escaped, with a certificate of such magistracy or other authority, as aforesaid, with the seal of the proper court or officer thereto attached, which seal shall be sufficient to establish the competency of the proof, and with proof, also by affidavit, of the identity of the person whose service or labor is claimed to be due as aforesaid, that the person so arrested does in fact owe service or labor to the person or persons claiming him or her, in the State or Territory from which such fugitive may have escaped as aforesaid, and that said person escaped, to make out and deliver to such claimant, his or her agent or attorney, a certificate setting forth the substantial facts as to the service or labor due from such fugitive to the claimant, and of his or her escape from the State or Territory in which he or she was arrested, with authority to such claimant, or his or her agent or attorney, to use such reasonable force and restraint as may be necessary, under the circumstances of the case, to take and remove such fugitive person back to the State or Territory whence he or she may have escaped as aforesaid. In no trial or hearing under this act shall the testimony of such alleged fugitive be admitted in evidence; and the certificates in this and the first [fourth] section mentioned, shall be conclusive of the right of the person or persons in whose favor granted, to remove such fugitive to the State or Territory from which he escaped, and shall prevent all molestation of such person or persons by any process issued by any court, judge, magistrate, or other person whomsoever.

Section 7: And be it further enacted, That any person who shall knowingly and willingly obstruct, hinder, or prevent such claimant, his agent or attorney, or any person or persons lawfully assisting him, her, or them, from arresting such a fugitive from service or labor, either with or without process as aforesaid, or shall rescue, or attempt to rescue, such fugitive from service or labor, from the custody of such claimant, his or her agent or attorney, or other person or persons lawfully assisting as aforesaid, when so arrested, pursuant to the authority herein given and declared; or shall aid, abet, or assist such person so owing service or labor as aforesaid, directly or indirectly, to escape from such claimant, his agent or attorney, or other person or persons legally authorized as aforesaid; or shall harbor or conceal such fugitive, so as to prevent the discovery and arrest of such person, after notice or knowledge of the fact that such person was a fugitive from service or labor as aforesaid, shall, for either of said offences, be subject to a fine not exceeding one thousand dollars, and imprisonment not exceeding six months, by indictment and conviction before the District Court of the United States for the district in which such offence may have been committed, or before the proper court of criminal jurisdiction, if committed within any one of the organized Territories of the United States; and shall moreover forfeit and pay, by way of civil damages to the party injured by such illegal conduct, the sum of one thousand dollars for each fugitive so lost as aforesaid, to be recovered by action of debt, in any of the District or Territorial Courts aforesaid, within whose jurisdiction the said offence may have been committed.

Section 8: And be it further enacted, That the marshals, their deputies, and the clerks of the said District and Territorial Courts, shall be paid, for their services, the like fees as may be allowed for similar services in other cases; and where such services are rendered exclusively in the arrest, custody, and delivery of the fugitive to the claimant, his or her agent or attorney, or where such supposed fugitive may be discharged out of custody for the want of sufficient proof as aforesaid, then such fees are to be paid in whole by such claimant, his or her agent or attorney; and in all cases where the proceedings are before a commissioner, he shall be entitled to a fee of ten dollars in full for his services in each case, upon the delivery of the said certificate to the claimant, his agent or attorney; or a fee of five dollars in cases where the proof shall not, in the opinion of such commissioner, warrant such certificate and delivery, inclusive of all services incident to such arrest and examination, to be paid, in either case, by the claimant, his or her agent or attorney. The person or persons authorized to execute the process to be issued by such commissioner for the arrest and detention of fugitives from service or labor as aforesaid, shall also be entitled to a fee of five dollars each for each person he or they may arrest, and take before any commissioner as aforesaid, at the instance and request of such claimant, with such other fees as may be deemed reasonable by such commissioner for such other additional services as may be necessarily performed by him or them; such as attending at the examination, keeping the fugitive in custody, and providing him with food and lodging during his detention, and until the final determination of such commissioners; and, in general, for performing such other duties as may be required by such claimant, his or her attorney or agent, or commissioner in the premises, such fees to be made up in conformity with the fees usually charged by the officers of the courts of justice within the proper district or county, as near as may be practicable, and paid by such claimants, their agents or attorneys, whether such supposed fugitives from service or labor be ordered to be delivered to such claimant by the final determination of such commissioner or not.

Section 9: And be it further enacted, That, upon affidavit made by the claimant of such fugitive, his agent or attorney, after such certificate has been issued, that he has reason to apprehend that such fugitive will he rescued by force from his or their possession before he can be taken beyond the limits of the State in which the arrest is made, it shall be the duty of the officer making the arrest to retain such fugitive in his custody, and to remove him to the State whence he fled, and there to deliver him to said claimant, his agent, or attorney. And to this end, the officer aforesaid is hereby authorized and required to employ so many persons as he may deem necessary to overcome such force, and to retain them in his service so long as circumstances may require. The said officer and his assistants, while so employed, to receive the same compensation, and to be allowed the same expenses, as are now allowed by law for transportation of criminals, to be certified by the judge of the district within which the arrest is made, and paid out of the treasury of the United States.:

Section 10: And be it further enacted, That when any person held to service or labor in any State or Territory, or in the District of Columbia, shall escape there from, the party to whom such service or labor shall be due, his, her, or their agent or attorney, may apply to any court of record therein, or judge thereof in vacation, and make satisfactory proof to such court, or judge in vacation, of the escape aforesaid, and that the person escaping owed service or labor to such party. Whereupon the court shall cause a record to be made of the matters so proved, and also a general description of the person so escaping, with such convenient certainty as may be; and a transcript of such record, authenticated by the attestation of the clerk and of the seal of the said court, being produced in any other State, Territory, or district in which the person so escaping may be found, and being exhibited to any judge, commissioner, or other office, authorized by the law of the United States to cause persons escaping from service or labor to be delivered up, shall be held and taken to be full and conclusive evidence of the fact of escape, and that the service or labor of the person escaping is due to the party in such record mentioned. And upon the production by the said party of other and further evidence if necessary, either oral or by affidavit, in addition to what is contained in the said record of the identity of the person escaping, he or she shall be delivered up to the claimant, And the said court, commissioner, judge, or other person authorized by this act to grant certificates to claimants or fugitives, shall, upon the production of the record and other evidences aforesaid, grant to such claimant a certificate of his right to take any such person identified and proved to be owing service or labor as aforesaid, which certificate shall authorize such claimant to seize or arrest and transport such person to the State or Territory from which he escaped: Provided, That nothing herein contained shall be construed as requiring the production of a transcript of such record as evidence as aforesaid. But in its absence the claim shall be heard and determined upon other satisfactory proofs, competent in law.

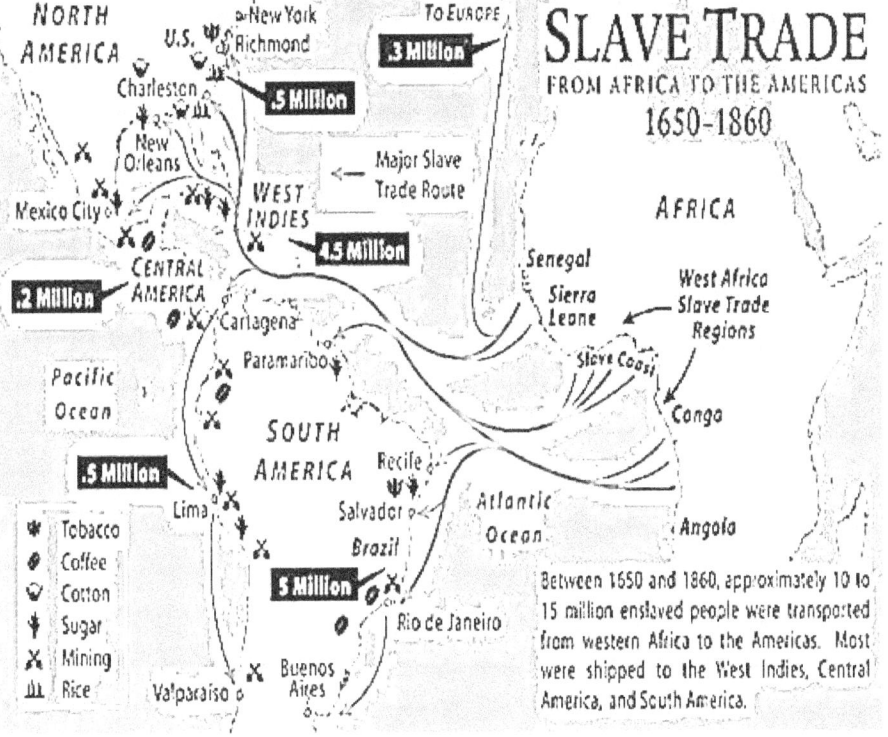

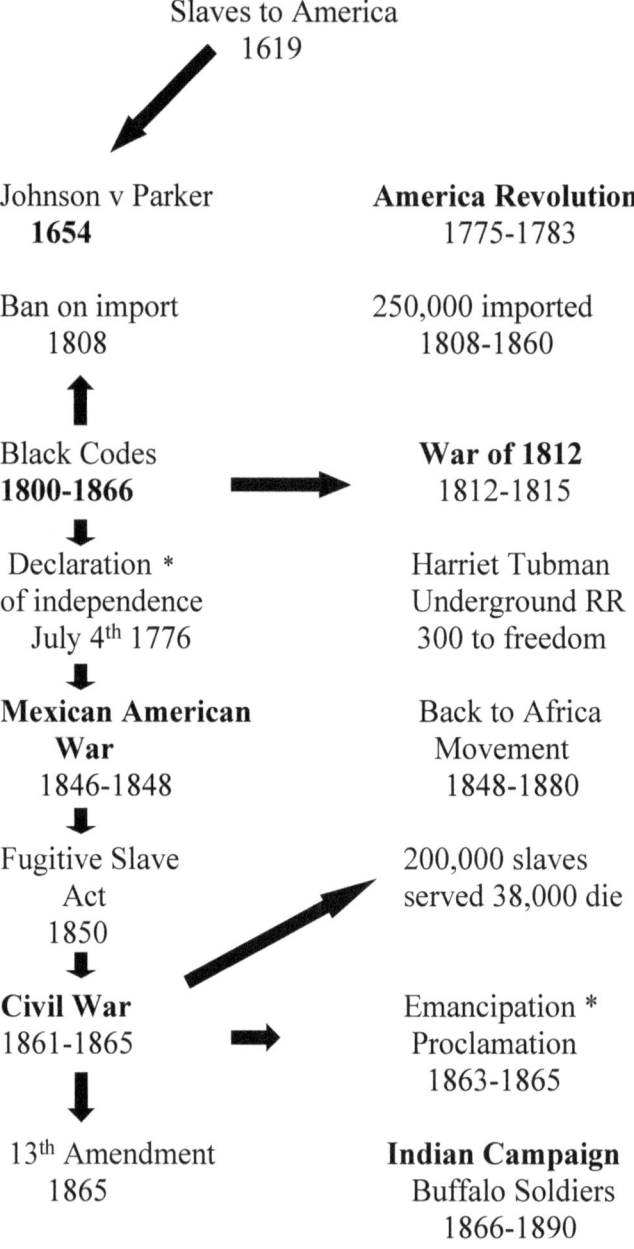

chart.1

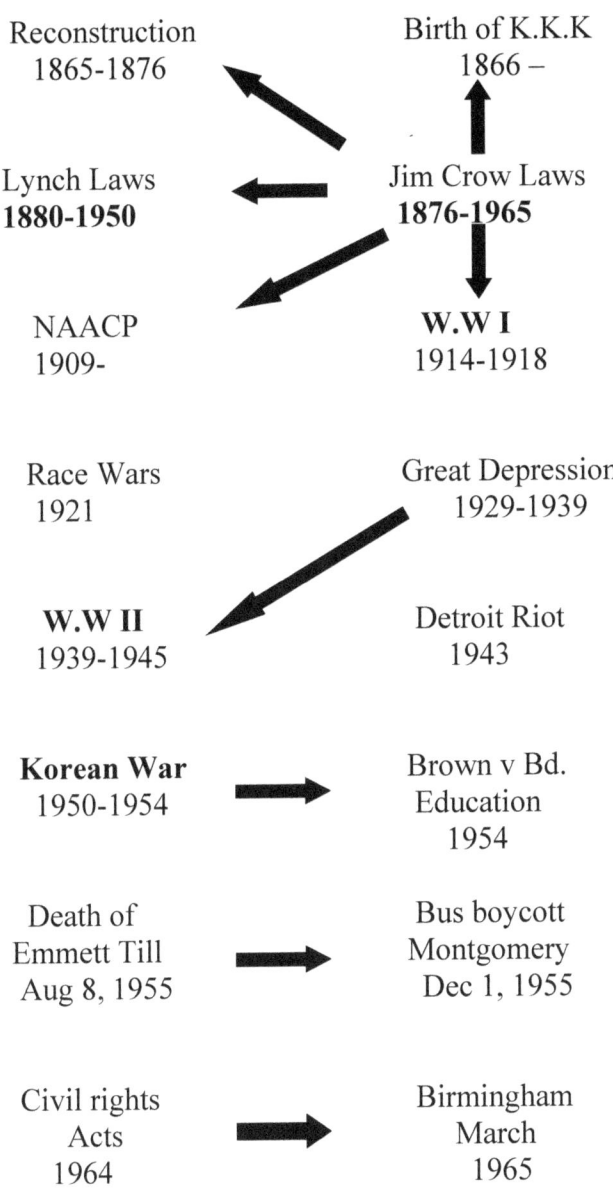

chart.2

Presidents During the Black Code Era

1800-1866

2. John Adams: 1797-1801.
3. Thomas Jefferson: 1801-1809
4. James Madison: 1809-1817
5. James Monroe: 1817-1825
6. John Quincy Adam: 1825-1829
7. Andrew Jackson: 1829-1837
8. Martin van Buren: 1837-1841
9. William Henry Harrison: 1841-1841
10. John Tyler: 1841-1845
11. James K. Polk: 1845-1849
12. Zachary Taylor: 1849-1850
13. Millard Fillmore: 1850-1853
14. Franklin Pierce: 1853-1857
15. James Buchanan: 1857-1861
16. Abraham Lincoln: 1861-1865
17. Andrew Johnson: 1865-1869

fig.1

Presidents During the Jim Crow Era

1876-1965

18. Ulysses S. Grant: 1869-1877
19. Rutherford B. Hayes: 1877-1881
20. James A. Garfield: 1881-1881
21. Chester A. Arthur: 1881-1885
22. Grover Cleveland: 1885-1889
23. Benjamin Harrison: 1889-1893
24. Grover Cleveland: 1893-1897
25. William McKinley: 1897-1901
26. Theodore Roosevelt: 1901-1909
27. William H. Taft: 1909-1913
28. Woodrow Wilson: 1913-1921
29. Warren G. Harding: 1921-1923
30. Calvin Coolidge: 1923-1929
31. Herbert C. Hoover: 1929-1933
32. Franklin D. Roosevelt: 1933-1945
33. Harry S. Truman: 1945-1953
34. Dwight D. Eisenhower: 1953-1961
35. John F. Kennedy: 1961-1963
36. Lyndon B. Johnson: 1963-1969

fig.2

Presidents During the Lynch Laws Era

1880-1950

19. Rutherford B. Hayes: 1877-1881
20. James A. Garfield: 1881-1881
21. Chester A. Arthur: 1881-1885
22. Grover Cleveland: 1885-1889
23. Benjamin Harrison: 1889-1893
24. Grover Cleveland: 1893-1897
25. William McKinley: 1897-1901
26. Theodore Roosevelt: 1901-1909
27. William H. Taft: 1909-1913
28. Woodrow Wilson: 1913-1921
29. Warren G. Harding: 1921-1923
30. Calvin Coolidge: 1923-1929
31. Herbert C. Hoover: 1929-1933
32. Franklin D. Roosevelt: 1933-1945
33. Harry S. Truman: 1945-1953

fig.3

Willie Lynch speech

Whether or not this was indeed a speech given by Willie Lynch is not certain, but this much is clear, what is stated here needs to be examined carefully as it is one of the many ways Black people have been controlled, it could very well be no more than propaganda but even propaganda has a bit of truth it takes its lessons from.

This speech was said to have been delivered by Willie Lynch on the bank of the James River in the colony of Virginia in 1712, you read it and draw your own conclusion. It is not a matter of when it was said but rather what is being said.

Be warned it is very graphic in nature.

Lynch was a British slave owner in the West Indies. He was invited to the colony of Virginia in 1712 to teach his methods to slave owners there. The term "lynching" is derived from his last name.
[beginning of the Willie Lynch Letter]

Greetings,

Gentlemen. I greet you here on the bank of the James River in the year of our Lord one thousand seven hundred and twelve. First, I shall thank you, the gentlemen of the Colony of Virginia, for bringing me here. I am here to help you solve some of your problems with slaves. Your invitation reached me on my modest plantation in the West Indies, where I have experimented with some of the newest, and still the oldest, methods for control of slaves. Ancient Rome would envy us if my program is implemented. As our boat sailed south on the James River, named for our illustrious King, whose version of the Bible we cherish, I saw enough to know that your problem is not unique. While Rome used cords of wood as crosses for standing human bodies along its highways in great numbers, you are here using the tree and the rope on occasions. I caught the whiff of a dead slave hanging from a tree, a couple miles back. You are not only losing valuable stock by hangings, you are having uprisings, slaves are running away, your crops are sometimes left in the fields too long for maximum profit, you suffer occasional fires, your animals are killed. Gentlemen, you know what your problems are; I do not need to elaborate. I am not here to enumerate your problems, I am here to introduce you to a method of solving them. In my bag here, I HAVE A FULL PROOF METHOD FOR CONTROLLING YOUR BLACK SLAVES. I guarantee every one of you that, if installed correctly, IT WILL CONTROL THE SLAVES FOR AT LEAST 300 HUNDREDS YEARS. My method is simple. Any member of your family or your overseer can use it. I HAVE OUTLINED A NUMBER OF DIFFERENCES AMONG THE SLAVES; AND I TAKE THESE DIFFERENCES AND MAKE THEM BIGGER. I USE FEAR, DISTRUST AND ENVY FOR CONTROL PURPOSES. These methods have worked on my modest plantation in the West Indies and it will work throughout the South. Take this simple little list of differences and think about them. On top of my list is "AGE," but it's there only because it starts with an "a." The second is "COLOR" or shade. There is INTELLIGENCE, SIZE, SEX, SIZES OF PLANTATIONS, STATUS on plantations, ATTITUDE of owners, whether the slaves live in the valley, on a hill, East, West, North,

South, have fine hair, course hair, or is tall or short. Now that you have a list of differences, I shall give you an outline of action, but before that, I shall assure you that DISTRUST IS STRONGER THAN TRUST AND ENVY STRONGER THAN ADULATION, RESPECT OR ADMIRATION. The Black slaves after receiving this indoctrination shall carry on and will become self-refueling and self-generating for HUNDREDS of years, maybe THOUSANDS. Don't forget, you must pitch the OLD black male vs. the YOUNG black male, and the YOUNG black male against the OLD black male. You must use the DARK skin slaves vs. the LIGHT skin slaves, and the LIGHT skin slaves vs. the DARK skin slaves. You must use the FEMALE vs. the MALE, and the MALE vs. the FEMALE. You must also have white servants and overseers [who] distrust all Blacks. But it is NECESSARY THAT YOUR SLAVES TRUST AND DEPEND ON US. THEY MUST LOVE, RESPECT AND TRUST ONLY US. Gentlemen, these kits are your keys to control. Use them. Have your wives and children use them, never miss an opportunity. IF USED INTENSELY FOR ONE YEAR, THE

SLAVES THEMSELVES WILL REMAIN PERPETUALLY DISTRUSTFUL. Thank you gentlemen."

LET'S MAKE A SLAVE

It was the interest and business of slave holders to study human nature, and the slave nature in particular, with a view to practical results. I and many of them attained astonishing proficiency in this direction. They had to deal not with earth, wood and stone, but with men and, by every regard, they had for their own safety and prosperity they needed to know the material on which they were to work, conscious of the injustice and wrong they were every hour perpetuating and knowing what they themselves would do. Were they the victims of such wrongs? They were constantly looking for the first signs of the dreaded retribution. They watched therefore with skilled and practiced eyes, and learned to read with great accuracy, the state of mind and heart of the slave, through his sable face. Unusual sobriety, apparent abstractions, sullenness and indifference indeed, any mood out of the common was afforded ground for suspicion and inquiry.

Frederick Douglas LET'S MAKE A SLAVE is a study of the scientific process of man-breaking and slave-making. It describes the rationale and results of the Anglo Saxons' ideas and methods of insuring the master/slave relationship. LET'S MAKE A SLAVE "The Original and Development of a Social Being Called 'The Negro.'" Let us make a slave. What do we need? First of all, we need a black nigger man, a pregnant nigger woman and her baby nigger boy. Second, we will use the same basic principle that we use in breaking a horse, combined with some more sustaining factors. What we do with horses is that we break them from one form of life to another; that is, we reduce them from their natural state in nature. Whereas nature provides them with the natural capacity to take care of their offspring, we break that natural string of independence from them and thereby create a dependency status, so that we may be able to get from them useful production for our business and pleasure.

CARDINAL PRINCIPLES FOR MAKING A NEGRO

For fear that our future generations may not understand the principles of breaking both of the beast together, the nigger and the horse. We understand that short range planning economics results in periodic economic chaos; so that to avoid turmoil in the economy, it requires us to have breadth and depth in long range comprehensive planning, articulating both skill sharp perceptions. We lay down the following principles for long range comprehensive economic planning. Both horse and niggers [are] no good to the economy in the wild or natural state. Both must be BROKEN and TIED together for orderly production. For orderly future, special and particular attention must be paid to the FEMALE and the YOUNGEST offspring. Both must be CROSSBRED to produce a variety and division of labor. Both must be taught to respond to a peculiar new LANGUAGE. Psychological and physical instruction of CONTAINMENT must be created for both. We hold the six cardinal principles as truth to be self-evident, based upon following the discourse concerning the economics of breaking and tying the horse and the nigger together, all inclusive of the six principles laid down above. NOTE: Neither principle alone will suffice for good economics. All principles must be employed for orderly good of the nation. Accordingly, both a wild horse and a wild or natur[al] nigger is dangerous even if captured, for they will have the tendency to seek their customary freedom and, in doing so, might kill you in your sleep. You cannot rest. They sleep while you are awake, and are awake while you are asleep. They are DANGEROUS near the family house and it requires too much labor to watch them away from the house. Above all, you cannot get them to work in this natural state. Hence, both the horse and the nigger must be broken; that is breaking them from one form of mental life to another, TAKE THE MIND! KEEP THE BODY In other words, break the will to resist. Now the breaking process is the same for both the horse and the nigger, only slightly varying in degrees. But, as we said before, there is an art in long range economic planning. YOU MUST KEEP YOUR EYE AND THOUGHTS ON THE FEMALE and the OFFSPRING of the horse and the nigger. A brief discourse in offspring development will shed light on the key to sound economic principles. Pay little attention to the generation of original breaking, but CONCENTRATE ON FUTURE GENERATION. Therefore, if you break the FEMALE mother, she will BREAK the offspring in its early years of development; and when the offspring is old enough to work, she will deliver it up to you, for her normal female protective tendencies will have been lost in the original breaking process. For example, take the case of the wild stud horse, a female horse and an already infant horse and compare the breaking process with two captured nigger males in their natural state, a pregnant nigger woman with her infant offspring. Take the stud horse, break him for limited containment. Completely break the female horse until she becomes very gentle, whereas you or anybody can ride her in her comfort. Breed the mare and the stud until you have the desired offspring. Then, you can turn the stud to freedom until you need him again. Train the female horse whereby she will eat out of your hand, and she will in turn train the infant horse to eat out of your hand, also. When it comes to breaking the uncivilized nigger, use the same process, but vary the degree and step up the pressure, so as to do a complete reversal of the mind. Take the meanest and most restless nigger, strip him of his clothes in front of the remaining male niggers, the female, and the nigger infant, tar and feather him, tie each leg to a different horse faced in opposite directions, set him afire and beat both horses to pull him apart in front of the remaining niggers. The next step is to take a bullwhip and beat the remaining nigger males to the point of death, in front of the female and the infant. Don't kill him, but PUT THE FEAR OF GOD IN HIM, for he can be useful for future breeding.

THE BREAKING PROCESS OF THE AFRICAN WOMAN

Take the female and run a series of tests on her to see if she will submit to your desires willingly. Test her in every way, because she is the most important factor for good economics. If she shows any sign of resistance in submitting completely to your will, do not hesitate to use the bullwhip on her to extract that last bit of [b----] out of her. Take care not to kill her, for in doing so, you spoil good economics. When in complete submission, she will train her offsprings in the early years to submit to labor when they become of age. Understanding is the best thing. Therefore, we shall go deeper into this area of the subject matter concerning what we have produced here in this breaking process of the female nigger. We have reversed the relationship; in her natural uncivilized state, she would have a strong dependency on the uncivilized nigger male, and she would have a limited protective tendency toward her independent male offspring and would raise male offsprings to be dependent like her. Nature had provided for this type of balance. We reversed nature by burning and pulling a civilized nigger apart and bullwhipping the other to the point of death, all in her presence. By her being left alone, unprotected, with the MALE IMAGE DESTROYED, the ordeal caused her to move from her psychologically dependent state to a frozen, independent state. In this frozen, psychological state of independence, she will raise her MALE and female offspring in reversed roles. For FEAR of the young male's life, she will psychologically train him to be MENTALLY WEAK and DEPENDENT, but PHYSICALLY STRONG. Because she has become psychologically independent, she will train her FEMALE offsprings to be psychologically independent. What have you got? You've got the nigger WOMAN OUT FRONT AND THE nigger MAN BEHIND AND SCARED. This is a perfect situation of sound sleep and economics. Before the breaking process, we had to be alertly on guard at all times. Now, we can sleep soundly, for out of frozen fear his woman stands guard for us. He cannot get past her early slave-molding process. He is a good tool, now ready to be tied to the horse at a tender age. By the time a nigger boy reaches the age of sixteen, he is soundly broken in and ready for a long life of sound and efficient work and the reproduction of a unit of good labor force. Continually through the breaking of uncivilized savage niggers, by throwing the nigger female savage into a frozen psychological state of independence, by killing the protective male image, and by creating a submissive dependent mind of the nigger male slave, we have created an orbiting cycle that turns on its own axis forever, unless a phenomenon occurs and re-shifts the position of the male and female slaves. We show what we mean by example. Take the case of the two economic slave units and examine them close.

THE NEGRO MARRIAGE

We breed two nigger males with two nigger females. Then, we take the nigger male away from them and keep them moving and working. Say one nigger female bears a nigger female and the other bears a nigger male; both nigger females—being without influence of the nigger male image, frozen with a independent psychology—will raise their offspring into reverse positions. The one with the female offspring will teach her to be like herself, independent and negotiable (we negotiate with her, through her, by her, negotiates her at will). The one with the nigger male offspring, she being frozen subconscious fear for his life, will raise him to be mentally dependent and weak, but physically strong; in other words, body over mind. Now, in a few years when these two offsprings become fertile for early reproduction, we will mate and breed them and continue the cycle. That is good, sound and long range comprehensive planning.

WARNING: POSSIBLE INTERLOPING NEGATIVES

Earlier, we talked about the non-economic good of the horse and the nigger in their wild or natural state; we talked out the principle of breaking and tying them together for orderly production. Furthermore, we talked about paying particular attention to the female savage and her offspring for orderly future planning, then more recently we stated that, by reversing the positions of the male and female savages, we created an orbiting cycle that turns on its own axis forever unless a phenomenon occurred and reshifts positions of the male and female savages. Our experts warned us about the possibility of this phenomenon occurring, for they say that the mind has a strong drive to correct and re-correct itself over a period of time if it can touch some substantial original historical base; and they advised us that the best way to deal with the phenomenon is to shave off the brute's mental history and create a multiplicity of phenomena of illusions, so that each illusion will twirl in its own orbit, something similar to floating balls in a vacuum. This creation of multiplicity of phenomena of illusions entails the principle of crossbreeding the nigger and the horse as we stated above, the purpose of which is to create a diversified division of labor; thereby creating different levels of labor and different values of illusion at each connecting level of labor. The results of which is the severance of the points of original beginnings for each sphere illusion. Since we feel that the subject matter may get more complicated as we proceed in laying down our economic plan concerning the purpose, reason and effect of crossbreeding horses and niggers, we shall lay down the following definition terms for future generations. Orbiting cycle means a thing turning in a given path. Axis means upon which or around which a body turns. Phenomenon means something beyond ordinary conception and inspires awe and wonder. Multiplicity means a great number. Means a globe. Crossbreeding a horse means taking a horse and breeding it with an ass and you get a dumb, backward, ass long-headed mule that is not reproductive nor productive by itself. Crossbreeding niggers mean taking so many drops of good white blood and putting them into as many nigger women as possible, varying the drops by the various tone that you want, and then letting them breed with each other until another circle of color appears as you desire. What this means is this: Put the niggers and the horse in a breeding pot, mix some asses and some good white blood and what do you get? You got a multiplicity of colors of ass backward, unusual niggers, running, tied to backward ass long-headed mules, the one productive of itself, the other sterile. (The one constant, the other dying, we keep the nigger constant for we may replace the mules for another tool) both mule and nigger tied to each other, neither knowing where the other came from and neither productive for itself, nor without each other.

CONTROLLED LANGUAGE

Crossbreeding completed, for further severance from their original beginning, WE MUST COMPLETELY ANNIHILATE THE MOTHER TONGUE of both the new nigger and the new mule, and institute a new language that involves the new life's work of both. You know language is a peculiar institution. It leads to the heart of a people. The more a foreigner knows about the language of another country the more he is able to move through all levels of that society. Therefore, if the foreigner is an enemy of the country, to the extent that he knows the body of the language, to that extent is the country vulnerable to attack or invasion of a foreign culture. For example, if you take a slave, if you teach him all about your language, he will know all your secrets, and he is then no more a slave, for you can't fool him any longer, and BEING A FOOL IS ONE OF THE BASIC INGREDIENTS OF ANY INCIDENTS TO THE MAINTENANCE OF THE SLAVERY SYSTEM. For example, if you told a slave that he must perform in getting out "our crops" and he knows the language well, he would know that "our crops" didn't mean "our crops" and the slavery system would break down, for he would relate on the basis of what "our crops" really meant. So you have to be careful in setting up the new language; for the slaves would soon be in your house, talking to you as "man to man" and that is death to our economic system. In addition, the definitions of words or terms are only a minute part of the process. Values are created and transported by communication through the body of the language. A total society has many interconnected value systems. All the values in the society have bridges of language to connect them for orderly working in the society. But for these language bridges, these many value systems would sharply clash and cause internal strife or civil war, the degree of the conflict being determined by the magnitude of the issues or relative opposing strength in whatever form. For example, if you put a slave in a hog pen and train him to live there and incorporate in him to value it as a way of life completely, the biggest problem you would have out of him is that he would worry you about provisions to keep the hog pen clean, or the same hog pen and make a slip and incorporate something in his language whereby he comes to value a house more than he does his hog pen, you got a problem. He will soon be in your house. Additional Note: "Henty Berry, speaking in the Virginia House of Delegates in 1832, described the situation as it existed in many parts of the South at this time: "We have, as far as possible, closed every avenue by which light may enter their (the slaves) minds. If we could extinguish the capacity to see the light, our work would be complete; they would then be on a level with the beasts of the field and we should be safe. I am not certain that we would not do it, if we could find out the process and that on the plea of necessity." From Brown America, The story of a New Race by Edwin R. Embree. 1931 The Viking Press.

Warning

Some of the following pictures you about to see may be disturbing. They are intended to be viewed by those who seek to understand American history as it relates to black people.

This is what was known as a slave pen, it was one of many holding areas that slaves were kept. Plantation owners would often pay for a slave in advance and be given a number that corresponded with the slave. After which they would be permitted to get their slave in what was called the **"grab and go"** method from these cells or pens as some of them were called.

$100 REWARD!

RANAWAY

From the undersigned, living on Current River, about twelve miles above Doniphan, in Ripley County, Mo., on 2nd of March, 1860, **A NEGRO MAN**, about 30 years old, weighs about 160 pounds; high forehead, with a scar on it; had on brown pants and coat very much worn, and an old black wool hat; shoes size No. 11.

The above reward will be given to any person who may apprehend this said negro out of the State; and fifty dollars if apprehended in this State outside of Ripley county, or $25 if taken in Ripley county.

APOS TUCKER.

Grandma Moses (Harriet Tubman) the leader of the Underground Railroad lead over 300 to freedom.

TO COLORED MEN!

FREEDOM,
Protection, Pay, and a Call to Military Duty!

On the 1st day of January, 1863, the President of the United States proclaimed FREEDOM to over THREE MILLIONS OF SLAVES. This decree is to be enforced by all the power of the Nation. On the 21st of July last he issued the following order:

PROTECTION OF COLORED TROOPS.

"WAR DEPARTMENT, ADJUTANT GENERAL'S OFFICE,
Washington, July 21.

"*General Order, No. 233.*

"The following order of the President is published for the information and government of all concerned:—

EXECUTIVE MANSION, WASHINGTON, July 30.

"'It is the duty of every Government to give protection to its citizens, of whatever class, color, or condition, and especially to those who are duly organized as soldiers in the public service. The law of nations, and the usages and customs of war, as carried on by civilized powers, permit no distinction as to color in the treatment of prisoners of war as public enemies. To sell or enslave any captured person on account of his color, is a relapse into barbarism, and a crime against the civilization of the age.

"'The Government of the United States will give the same protection to all its soldiers, and if the enemy shall sell or enslave any one because of his color, the offence shall be punished by retaliation upon the enemy's prisoners in our possession. It is, therefore, ordered, for every soldier of the United States, killed in violation of the laws of war, a rebel soldier shall be executed; and for every one enslaved by the enemy, or sold into slavery, a rebel soldier shall be placed at hard labor on the public works, and continued at such labor until the other shall be released and receive the treatment due to prisoners of war.

"ABRAHAM LINCOLN."

"'By order of the Secretary of War.
"E. D. TOWNSEND, Assistant Adjutant General.'"

That the President is in earnest the rebels soon began to find out, as witness the following order from his Secretary of War:

"WAR DEPARTMENT, WASHINGTON CITY, August 3, 1863.

"SIR: Your letter of the 3d inst., calling the attention of this Department to the cases of Orin H. Brown, William H. Johnston, and Wm. Wilson, three colored men captured on the gunboat Isaac Smith, has received consideration. This Department has directed that three rebel prisoners of South Carolina, if there be any such in our possession, and if not, three others, be confined in close custody and held as hostages for Brown, Johnston and Wilson, and that the fact be communicated to the rebel authorities at Richmond.

"Very respectfully your obedient servant,
"EDWIN M. STANTON, Secretary of War."

"The Hon. GIDEON WELLES, Secretary of the Navy."

And retaliation will be our practice now—man for man—to the bitter end.

LETTER OF CHARLES SUMNER,
Written with reference to the Convention held at Poughkeepsie, July 15th and 16th, 1863, to promote Colored Enlistments.

BOSTON, July 13th, 1863.

"I doubt if, in times past, our country could have expected from colored men any patriotic service. Such service is the return for protection. But now that protection has begun, the service should begin also. Nor should relative rights and duties be weighed with nicety. It is enough that our country, aroused at last to a sense of justice, seeks to enrol colored men among its defenders.

"If my counsels should reach such persons, I would say: enlist at once. Now is the day and now is the hour. Help to overcome your cruel enemies now battling against your country, and in this way you will surely overcome those other enemies hardly less cruel, here at home, who will still seek to degrade you. This is not the time to hesitate or to higgle. Do your duty to our country, and you will set an example of generous self-sacrifice which will conquer prejudice and open all hearts.

"Very faithfully yours,
"CHARLES SUMNER."

Although blacks were lured into the military with promises of freedom and equality it would never take place.

The Black Soldier. It really didn't matter what side he fought on, he was not looked upon as a true soldier.

Blacks were given the grim task of collecting the remains of the dead. Blacks were instructed to recover the bodies of white soldiers who were given military funerals with honors. Black soldiers recovered were thrown into mass graves.

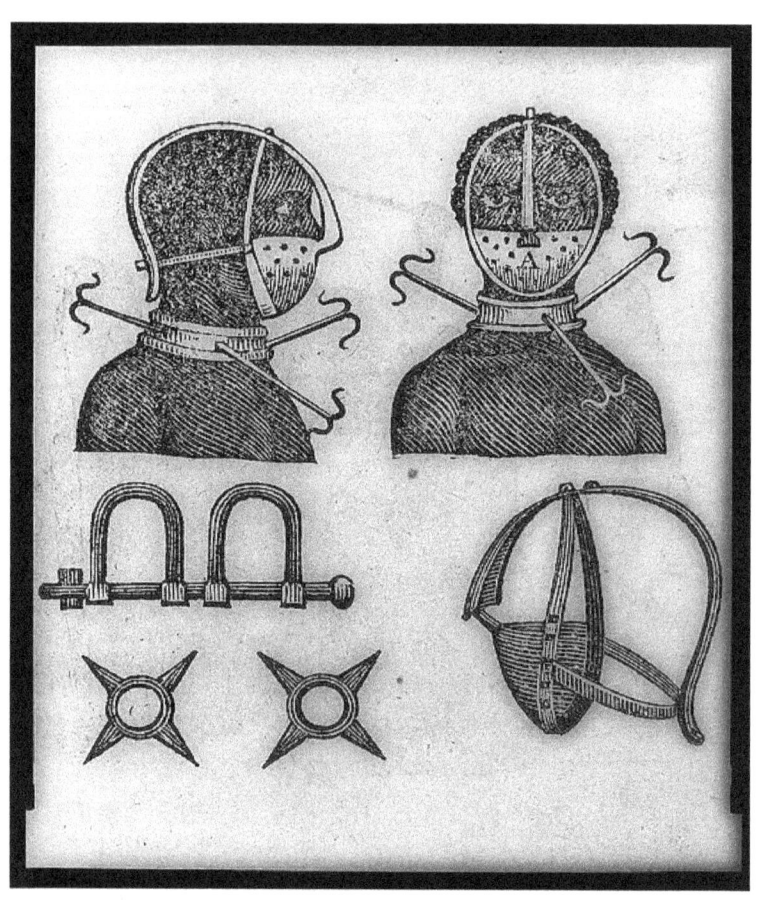

The tools of slavery were barbaric, and humiliating.

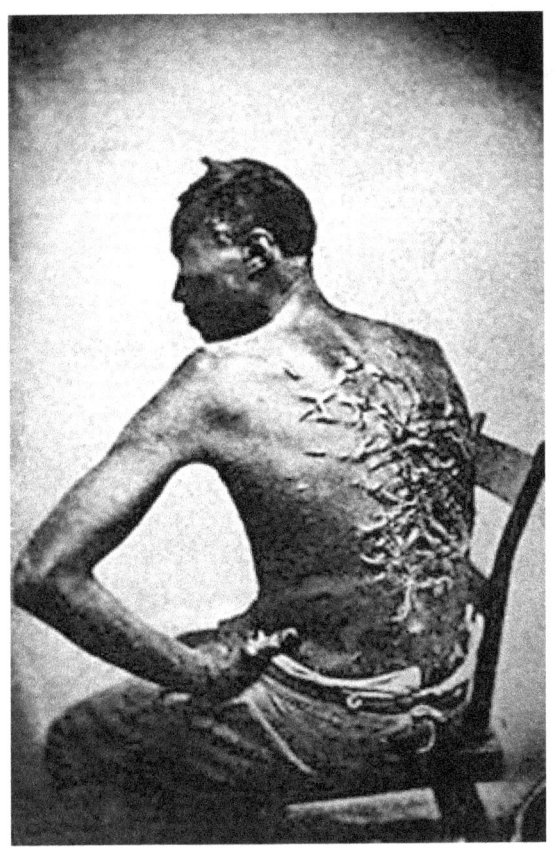

Someone once said that black people will not work; you have to force them to do so. Blacks worked seven days a week from sun up to often long after sundown, even after being beaten. They were not lives they were property.

Blacks have no feelings or emotions like real people so you can do what you want to them.

Surviving did not mean living.

A slave's life was not a happy life. It was work from sun up to sundown, and if they could provide for their own families or children.

Look at his eyes. Here is a man who knows he is moments away from death, yet remains strong.

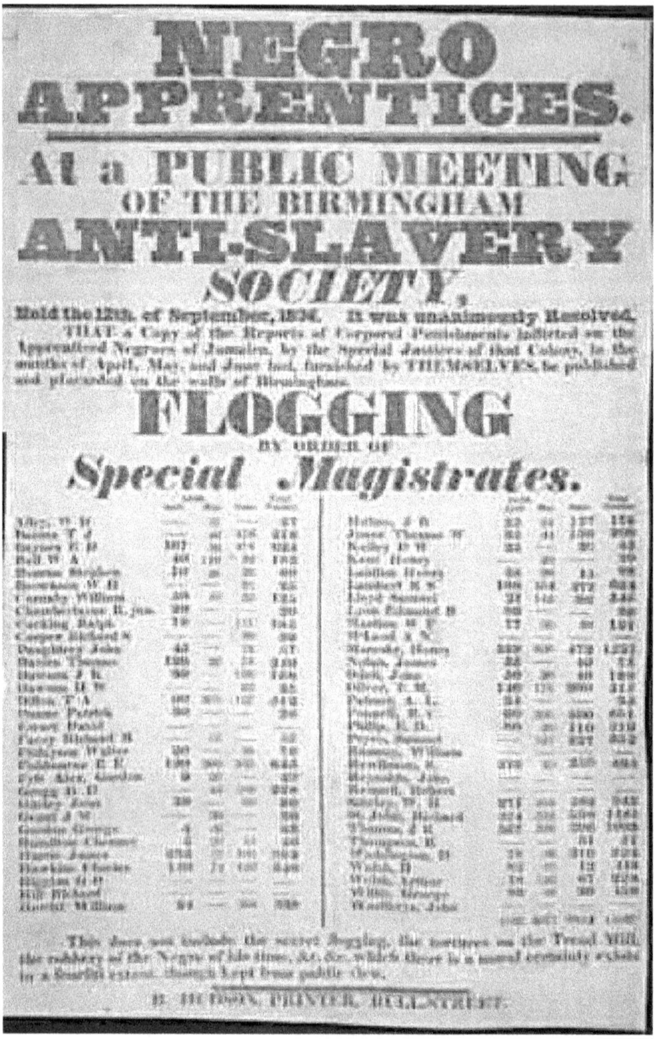

NEGRO APPRENTICES.

At a PUBLIC MEETING OF THE BIRMINGHAM ANTI-SLAVERY SOCIETY,

Held the 12th. of September, 1836. It was unanimously Resolved, THAT a Copy of the Reports of Corporal Punishments inflicted on the Apprenticed Negroes of Jamaica, by the Special Justices of that Colony, in the months of April, May, and June last, furnished by THEMSELVES, be published and placarded on the walls of Birmingham.

FLOGGING BY ORDER OF Special Magistrates.

[Table of names and figures, largely illegible]

This does not include the secret flogging, the tortures on the Tread Mill, the robbery of the Negro of his time, &c. &c. which there is a moral certainty exists to a fearful extent, though kept from public view.

B. HUDSON, PRINTER, BULL-STREET.

A slave bell collar was used for the overseer to know where a slave was on the plantation.

Slave Families

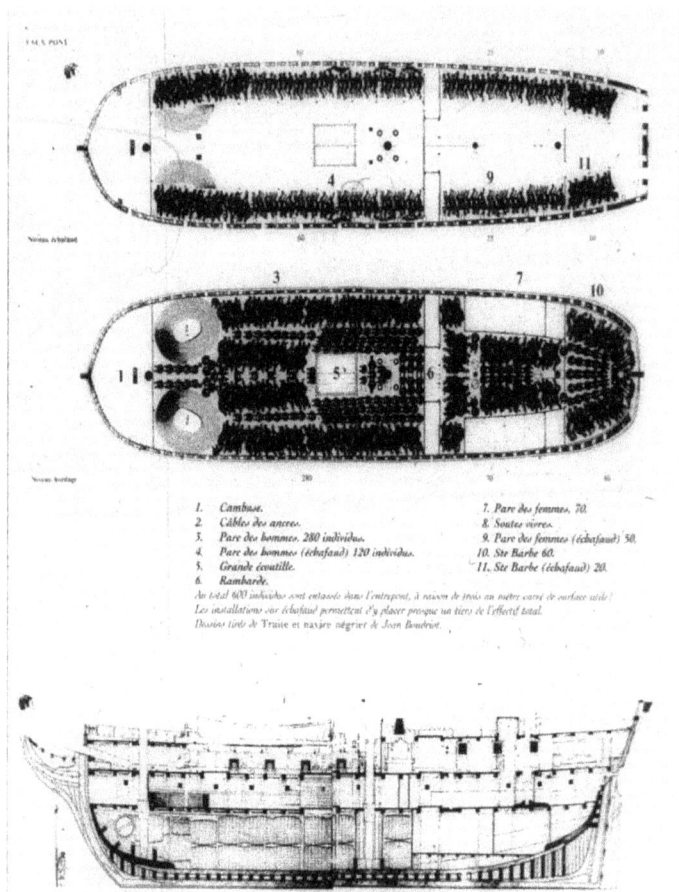

Slave ships were not built for comfort. Every available space was used to place slaves. The smell was sickening, and disease often claimed more than half of the slaves imported.

Children On Board Slave Ships

When it was said that slaves had no souls, it was due to them never having moments of peace. Look at this mans eyes; these are the eyes that have lost hope.

Freed slaves could not always find work.

Many deaths of blacks were due to Jim Crow laws.

One of the most brutal things white people did to black people was lynching…

The murder of blacks was so popular that school kids took pictures with the bodies.

They could happen on any day.

Over 15,000 would attend a lynching of black person, even selling seats for 5 cents

They could include men, women…

and children….

14 yr old Emmett Till prior to his death in August of 1955.

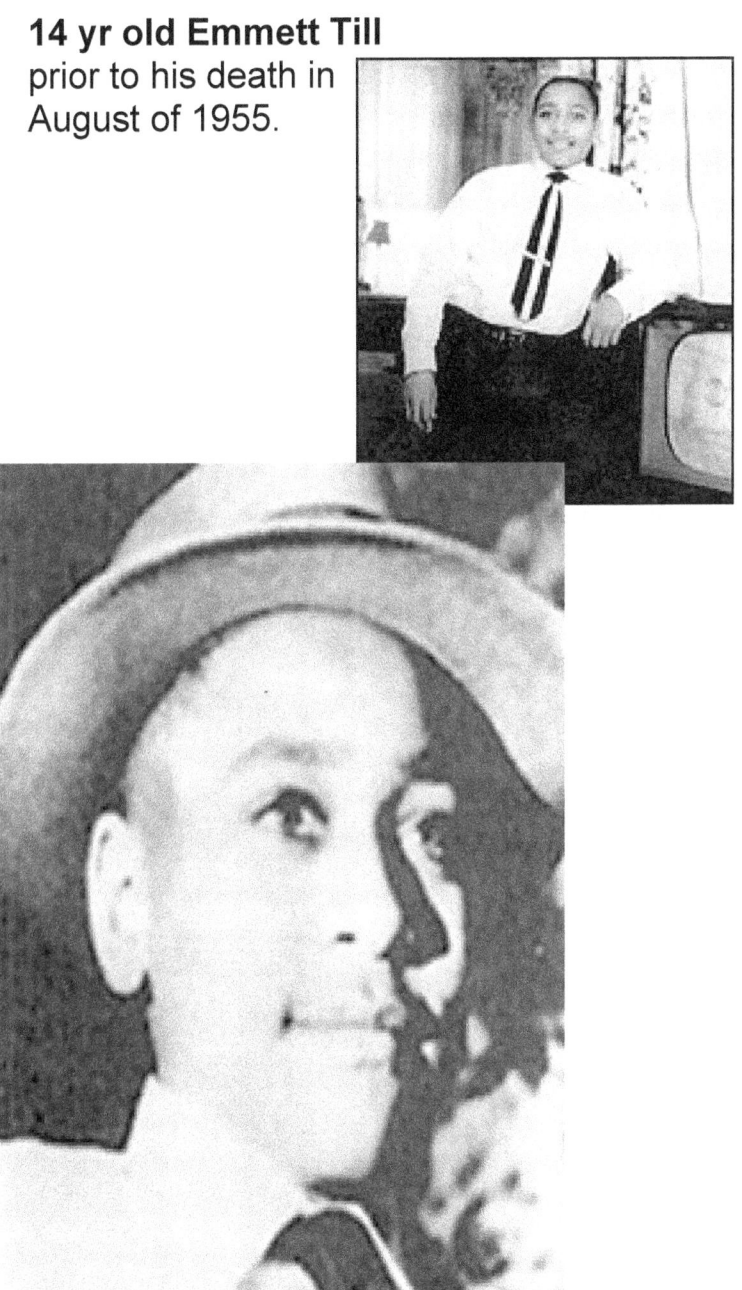

Photo of Emmett Till one month later, in September of 1955.

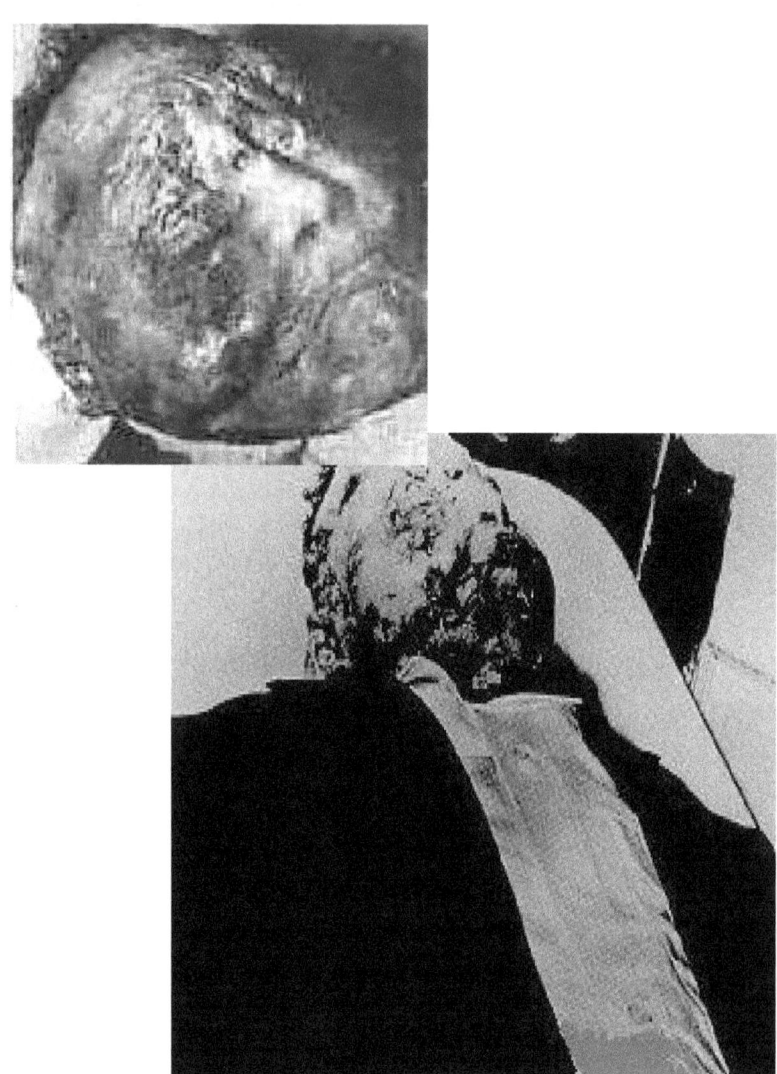

NOTES

Conclusion

Was this the first Holocaust, certainly not, but by far it was one of the countries worse.

Blacks have suffered longer than any other race of people, but they have not been the only race to suffer at the hands of a people who seek domination over other races.

This book is just an introduction into to the vial imagination of men's hearts. Millions have died at the hands of fearful men. Will there ever be an apology given to black people for the things done to them?

Will we continue to hear that it was our fathers sins not ours? If this is truly believed, then why does racism continue today? Why are blacks still being singled out above all other race of people? Why is there still higher unemployment among black people?

Questions upon questions will not be answered, when all we hear is it is not our fault. America's wealth is in the hands of greedy men who obtained that wealth through the brutality of slavery.

Slavery continues today in some form around the world. Slave labor still exists, and Jim Crow is as real today as it has ever been.

Things will not truly change until hearts change and hearts are not about to change anytime soon.

That's my nigga!
Nigga please!
Niggers are trash!
I hate Niggers! (aka Niggars)

We hear these terms spoken by both blacks as well as whites. The attempt is to make the word less offensive through general use. It loses its power supposedly the more it is used. That however is not true; some of us have simply become jaded by its use. Those who are 30 years old and younger have no real working knowledge of the offensiveness of the word and have no issue with using it. Even sadder are those who are older using the word with total disregard for the history of black people. It is those who do know the history of its usage toward black people that see the harm in its use.

So what's in a word? What's all the fuss, it's just a word, it's time that old people move on, young people have. There is only one problem with that. Young people are moving on from what? Have they suffered, been abused or dogs let loose on them? Have young people today, watched as their family members were murdered and called niggars? Maybe they should use the word because they know what it's like to have loved ones pulled from their bed in the midnight hour, pistol whipped, beaten, and then castrated while being called niggar. Maybe this was their way of becoming friends.

Four hundred years of being called niggar and the best we can do is say it is not a bad term. We don't mean it the way they (slave masters, overseers, and white people in general) did, it's just a playful term used by buddies and friends.

Maybe four hundred years of oppression did not exist. To be a niggar means to be my friend. Niggar is seen as black, dark without a soul, not human and as property. Maybe in one generation young people got it right and all the word needed was a makeover. All that was needed was for young men and women to simply forget their families past, the millions of black men, women and children who were slaughtered and butchered for not accepting their position as niggars.

A black person using the word Niggar is not offensive to white people. Whites used it towards blacks for hundreds of years to keep blacks in their place. When black people use the word niggar it is done to offend other black people. We have been taught how to effectively disrespect blacks as a race of people. We now have "black to black" racism. The youth of today would rather live a life filled with video games, dance to the music of iTunes and iPads than to face the reality that a little word like niggar cast a great shadow in the history of Black Americans.

"My Niggas"

(Written By Andrew C. White)

In the streets when we speak
we say those "My Nigga's"
but a couple hundred years ago
refusing to see the bigger picture
slave masters by the masses
had blacks picking cotton
saying those "My Niggers"

but not just the white man
the black Kings and Queens from
the motherland
chose "My Nigga's"
packaged them up like product
and sold "My Nigga's"

put a price on their souls
for trades of gold and promises of
40acres and a mule "My Nigga's"
to mislead and confuse "My
Nigga's"

but in the streets when we speak
we say those "My Nigga's"
even though in 1955 Dr. Martin
Luther King
joined the boycott scene

so we wouldn't be "No Nigga's"

so think about the blacks that
were attacked by dogs, bullets and
 bats
sprayed with fire hoses, locked in
 prisons
 and called "Niggers"

so you see the next time you want
to be "My Nigga's"
Just wait a cotton picking minute
and be the name you were
 given...............

Used by permission

Upcoming Releases
By: Timothy White, Sr.

The Evil That's me
The truth about why bad things happen to good people.

The Lord's Prayer
A verse by verse study of the real Lord's Prayer

The Truth Was Revealed in the Upper Room
A look at the events of the upper room from a unique perspective.

The Truth About Lies and Those Who Tell Them
Do saints tell the truth all the time, can you spot a liar, and are you a liar?

Just A Thought
370 thoughts that will get you through the year, and challenge you along the way.

Pulpit Pimps and Their Power to Deceive
Everyone who claims the word of God, and boast to be sent by the Lord is not telling the truth, how can we know…?

You Might Remember Me, but You Really Don't Know Me
Some of the most dangerous people are those who spend the most time with us. The reason for this is simple; they often know the most about us, or do they?

How do I know when God is talking to me?
Can we really be sure when God is talking to us, or is it just our imagination, of wishful thinking. There is a way you can be certain.

The Fearful Giver
Are we giving according to what the word of God says, there is more to giving than leaving money...

www.ingramcontent.com/pod-product-compliance
Lightning Source LLC
Chambersburg PA
CBHW032037150426
43194CB00006B/315